What Place for
Hunter-Gatherers
in Millennium Three?

SIL International
International Museum of Cultures
Publications in Ethnography

Publication 38

Publications in Ethnography (formerly International Museum of Cultures Series) is a series published jointly by SIL International and the International Museum of Cultures. The series focuses on cultural studies of minority peoples of various parts of the world. While most volumes are authored by members of SIL International who have done ethnologic research in minority languages, suitable works by others will also occasionally form part of the series.

Series Editor
David C. Wakefield

Volume Editors
Thomas N. Headland and Doris E. Blood

Production Staff
Bonnie Brown, Managing Editor
Mae Zook, Compositor
Kirby O'Brien, Photo Artist and Cover Design

What Place for Hunter-Gatherers in Millennium Three?

Edited by:
Thomas N. Headland
and Doris E. Blood

with a Foreword by Alan Barnard

SIL International
and
International Museum of Cultures
Dallas, Texas

©2002 by SIL International
Library of Congress Catalog No: 2002108759
ISBN: 1-55671-132-8
ISSN: 0-0895-9897

Printed in the United States of America

All Rights Reserved

06 05 04 03 02   7 6 5 4 3 2 1

The photograph on the front cover illustrates the theme of this volume. It is a depiction of an Agta man sitting on the top of a skyscraper, staring in wonderment out over the city of Manila. A similar photograph was used for the large color photomural (7 ft. by 8 ft. square) that stood at the entrance into the Agta Exhibit in the International Museum of Cultures throughout the year 2000. It was a favorite photo among the visitors because it vividly depicts the dilemma of the Agta and other hunting and gathering peoples today as their lands are taken from them and turned into croplands and industrial enterprises. Photo artist Kirby O'Brien created this mural by superimposing a 1963 photograph of an Agta man on top of a photo of the Makati district of Manila, the capital city of the Philippines.

Dedicated to the memory of
Eleden Aduanan
(born about 1931, died March 30, 2002)
Best friend, teacher, guide, advisor, respected Agta leader, and
trusted and true uncle to the Headlands' three children

Eleden Aduanan in 1994

Contents

Tables

Figures

Foreword

I have long argued that two kinds of comparison are useful in anthropology. The first is careful, controlled comparison within a geographical or ethnographic region, to narrow the range of variables (by analogy with a chemistry or physics experiment) and ensure that we are comparing like to like. The second is comparison of one region to another. This book has both. The studies of the Agta and neighboring groups (examined by Bion Griffin and Thomas Headland), of Philippine hunter-gatherers more widely, and to some extent of the South East Asian hunter-gatherers in general, represent the first. The comparisons to southern African hunter-gatherers (the various San or Bushman groups examined by Robert Hitchcock) and central African Efe hunter-gatherers and the Lese farmers who reside in close proximity (examined by Robert Bailey), represent the second type of comparison. Environmental degradation (highlighted herein by Sy Sohmer and Ben Wallace), economic transition, outside pressures and outside assistance, and the growth of indigenous human rights organizations, have all had similar and literally comparable effects (negative and positive) on the peoples described in this volume. Through comparison, great awareness can come.

In my own research area, the Kalahari Desert, and especially the central-western Kalahari areas inhabited by the Nharo (Naro) people, has seen radical changes over the last thirty years or so. In the early 1970s, most Nharo were living on vast ranches. Nevertheless, a great many Nharo, even in the interior of the ranching area, were capable of hunting and gathering and many still gathered for much of their subsistence. In the late 1970s and through the 1980s, drought brought greater dependence on outside resources. Ultimately, a whole generation and more grew up without the knowledge of wild plants, and therefore without the ability to gather. Game was already scarce in the ranching area, and it grew scarcer to the south of that area as well. By the time of my early fieldwork, many Nharo had taken to herding their own livestock, especially goats, and they tended cattle for white ranchers as well as Kgalagadi and Herero subsistence pastoralists.

The Agta number some 11,000 people. The Nharo are very similar in number. The Nharo language is perhaps less under threat than that of the Agta, and indeed has been given a great boost with the recent publication, by SIL International, of a substantial new dictionary. Yet, the Nharo too have seen a loss of land and a stifling of self-determination over the last century or more, with European settlement in their area. Their "transition phase" (as John Early and Headland have called it for the Agta), between foraging and peasant life, is lasting longer than that of the Agta. The Kuru Development Trust has been helping to preserve the Nharo language (they prefer the spelling *Naro*) and teach literacy by using it. Kuru, funded by Reformed Churches in the Netherlands, along with indigenous organizations like First People of the Kalahari, have put forward a diversity of programs to aid the economic development of the Nharo and other impoverished and dispossessed groups. For me, as a Nharo ethnographer, I find the Agta story particularly interesting both in its parallels and in differences with the situation among Nharo and their neighbors, the better-known G/wi of the central Kalahari and Ju/'hoansi (!Kung) of the northern Kalahari.

As Thomas Headland says, "Culture change is not always bad." The future well-being of the Agta, the Nharo and other former foragers depends on cultural awareness and self-determination, not on the preservation of specific economic activities as the sole means of making a living. If the human rights of proud foraging and former foraging peoples are given the attention they deserve, then there can be a bright future for them in Millennium Three and beyond. That said, the task is not an easy one, but this book will help greatly to focus our attention on the issues that matter.

Alan Barnard

Professor of the Anthropology of Southern Africa
University of Edinburgh
Edinburgh,   Scotland

Preface

The International Museum of Cultures (IMC) is an independent not-for-profit corporation affiliated with SIL International. Initiated in 1974 and incorporated in 1979, its mission is "to be a window on indigenous peoples of the world and to create greater appreciation for ethnic and cultural diversity, thereby furthering mutual respect and peace between peoples." It purposes (a) to disseminate knowledge concerning the rich cultural diversity and creativity existing in today's world, with special reference to linguistic groups living at the margins of life as we know it; (b) to support programs of teaching, research, and publication which will contribute to the well-being of the aforementioned linguistic groups; and (c) to promote peace and mutual respect between persons and groups of differing cultural and linguistic origins, both locally and internationally.

The first of a series of projected galleries opened in 1981. From this gallery emanate exhibitions and cultural programs that feature the culture and arts of contemporary indigenous peoples. Most IMC exhibitions draw upon the extensive intellectual resources of SIL International whose researchers have intimate cultural and language-related knowledge of hundreds of such groups. One area of the Museum's gallery is dedicated to short-term exhibitions that usually show for nine or ten months, a new major exhibit appearing every year.

In January 1999, I asked my SIL colleague, Thomas Headland, to assist in designing and developing a one-year museum exhibition for the 2000 season, to feature the Agta people of the Philippines. As one of only a few remaining "tribal" societies on our planet, in the true anthropological sense of this word, the Agta provide a final glimpse of a people who, within our lifetime, have practiced a true hunting-and-gathering lifestyle. The Agta are also fascinating because, being very short in stature and very dark-complexioned, they differ noticeably in physical makeup from other indigenous peoples of the Philippines. They descend from the archipelago's earliest inhabitants. Finally, our generation has witnessed—and participated in—the virtual destruction of their traditional rainforest habitat, which forced them into dramatic and very rapid cultural change during the last half of the twentieth century. The abundant habitat of days gone by has been stripped, and the grandchildren of accomplished hunter-gatherers, for lack of game, no longer know how to hunt.

Headland, a trained anthropologist who lived with his family among the Agta for most of his adult life, was the logical person to help with this exhibit. In addition to providing intellectual and artifactual resources, Tom helped us contact others who participated with us to make the project a success. Chief among those was Dr. P. Bion Griffin, Tom's mentor at the University of Hawai'i.

Almost all of the graphic material that appeared in the exhibit, as well as sup-
porting documentation, came from these two men.

SIL colleagues Monie and MariAnne Chiong, and Joe and Grace McAlpin,
who are also engaged in field programs among Agta peoples, assisted in the collection of artifacts and, along with Filipinos Nard Pugyao and James Daguman,
provided valuable counsel on exhibit production. These and others from the
Philippine-American community in North Texas formed an Advisory Council to
assist in exhibit planning. The Dallas members of this council were Filipinos
Mrs. Emelita D. de la Rosa and Mr. Galileo R. Jumao-as.

Tom's son, Steve Headland, reassembled the Agta lean-to that an Agta
family had created for us. Volunteer artist Lorette Brown, of Saskatoon, Sas-
katchewan, Canada, sculpted the Agta manikin firemaker (photo on page xxii)
and shared her expertise in other aspects of the artistic presentation of the
exhibition. Kirby O'Brien created photomurals and helped with other graphics.
Hyatt Moore created and donated several original paintings.

Financial sponsors of the exhibition included SIL International, the City of
Dallas Office of Cultural Affairs, the Texas Commission on the Arts, the Dallas
Morning News, the Philippines Program of SIL International, BankOne Texas,
and the general membership of the Museum.

Finally, this volume reflects one of the most rewarding aspects of the
exhibition, the public lectures that featured an outstanding group of experts on
hunter-gatherers such as the Agta and on the human and ecological challenges
associated with the industrialized world's modern assault on rainforest habitats.
The credit for assembling this fine panel of experts must go to Headland and to
Eileen McKee of the Museum staff, who assisted him. Special thanks are due to
the Anthropology Department of Southern Methodist University for their partnership with the Museum in sponsoring one of these events, the lecture series at
SMU on September 25, 2000, where the main papers in this volume were first
presented.

William R. Merrifield

Director Emeritus

International Museum of Cultures

Dallas, Texas

Contributors

ROBERT BAILEY (Ph.D. in anthropology, Harvard University and a MPH in Epidemiology, Emory University) is Professor of Epidemiology and Anthropology at University of Illinois at Chicago. His research interests are human behavioral ecology, growth, nutrition, HIV/AIDS prevention, and the interface between conservation ecology and indigenous peoples' needs. In 1980 he founded the Ituri Project, an interdisciplinary research and community development project in northeast Democratic Republic of Congo. His publications include *The Behavioral Ecology of Efe Men in the Ituri Forest, Zaire, Efe: Investigating Food and Fertility in the Ituri Forest* (with Nadine Peacock), and *Tropical Deforestation: The Human Dimension* (edited with Leslie Sponsel and Thomas Headland).

ALAN BARNARD (Ph.D. in anthropology, University of London) is Professor of the Anthropology of Southern Africa, University of Edinburgh, Scotland. His research interests include kinship, settlement patterns, images and self-images of hunter-gatherers, and the history of anthropology. He has done fieldwork with hunter-gatherers, former hunter-gatherers, and herders in Botswana, Namibia, and South Africa and has served as a social development advisor to the British government. His books include *Hunters and Herders of Southern Africa; History and Theory in Anthropology;* and *Social Anthropology,* and his edited books include the *Encyclopedia of Social and Cultural Anthropology* (with Jonathan Spencer) and *Africa's Indigenous Peoples* (with Justin Kenrick). Together with Tim Ingold, he is co-convener of the Ninth International Conference on Hunting and Gathering Societies, Edinburgh, September 2002.

DORIS BLOOD (M.A. in anthropology, University of Texas at Arlington) has been the editor of SIL's journal, *Notes on Anthropology.* Her first fieldwork experience was in a Mamanwa village with Philippine Negritos on Mindanao for eighteen months in 1957–1958. She later worked with her husband, David Blood, in linguistics and literacy for the Cham people of South Vietnam (1958–1975), and subsequently with the Lotud Dusun people of Sabah, Malaysia (1984–1993). Her publications include "The 'Y' Archiphoneme in Mamanwa," in *Anthropological Linguistics* in 1962, *Tales from Indochina* (coeditor with Marilyn Gregerson et al., 1987), and "The Lotud" (in *Social Organization of Sabah Societies,* Sherwood Lingenfelter, ed., 1990).

BION GRIFFIN (Ph.D. in anthropology, University of Arizona) is Professor of Anthropology and Associate Dean, College of Social Sciences, University of Hawai'i at Manoa. His primary interests are the anthropology of Southeast Asia, with special attention to the Philippines and Cambodia, the material culture and subsistence of small-scale societies, and the ethnography of food. Since 1972 he has maintained a research program among the Agta of northeastern Luzon, the Philippines. Special interests among the Agta include gender-based behaviors and technology. He edited, along with Agnes Estioko-Griffin, *The Agta of Northeastern Luzon: Recent Studies.* He has published numerous articles on the Agta and on Cambodian archaeology.

THOMAS HEADLAND (Ph.D. in anthropology, University of Hawai'i) is an international anthropology consultant with SIL International, adjunct professor of linguistics at the University of Texas at Arlington, and visiting professor at the University of North Dakota. His primary research interest is in tropical forest human ecology. From 1962, he spent eighteen years living in the Philippine rainforest with Agta hunter-gatherer people, with his most recent fieldwork there being in the spring of 2002. Among his books is *The Tasaday Controversy: Assessing the Evidence,* published by the American Anthropological Association, and *Tropical Deforestation,* coedited with Leslie Sponsel and Robert Bailey. He was the chief consultant and advisor for the year 2000 museum exhibit at the International Museum of Cultures (in Dallas, Texas) titled "The Philippine Agta: Their Rainforest is Gone: What Now?" He was also the chair at the colloquium at Southern Methodist University in September 2000, where the papers in this volume were first presented.

ROBERT HITCHCOCK (Ph.D. in anthropology, University of New Mexico) is Professor of Anthropology and Geography, the Coordinator of Conflict and Resolution Studies, and the Coordinator of African Studies at the University of Nebraska-Lincoln. His primary research interests are human rights of indigenous peoples, human ecology, and the impacts of development on hunter-gatherer and pastoral societies. He has lived and worked in Africa for over a dozen years. He is the author of *Kalahari Communities: Bushmen and the Politics of the Environment in Southern Africa* and is coeditor of *Hunter-Gatherers in the Modern World: Conflict, Resistance, and Self-Determination.* A member of the Panel of Environmental Experts for the Lesotho Highlands Water Project, Africa's largest contemporary development project, Prof. Hitchcock continues to work on development, human rights, and environmental issues in Africa, the Middle East, the Pacific, and North America.

WILLIAM MERRIFIELD (Ph.D. in cultural anthropology, Cornell University), now retired, served with SIL International for forty-seven years in a variety of roles: field linguist among the Palantla Chinantec people (Mexico), SIL School Director (University of Oklahoma and University of Washington), Founding Director of the International Museum of Cultures, and SIL International Coordinator for Anthropology, Community Development, and Academic Publications. He held adjunct or summer appointments at several universities, including the University of Texas at Arlington, where he was a full member of the Graduate Faculty. He has coauthored or coedited twelve academic books and over forty journal articles. His most recent 1999 book, coedited with Alfred Anderson, is the 760-page *Diccionario Chinanteco de la Diáspora del Pueblo Antiguo de San Pedro Tlatepuzco Oaxaca,* a forty-year research project funded in part by a grant from the National Science Foundation.

S. H. ("SY") SOHMER (Ph.D. in botany, University of Hawai'i) is President and Director of the Botanical Research Institute of Texas (BRIT). He was the senior biodiversity advisor for the Agency for International Development from 1990 to 1993, and chairman of the Botany Department of the Bernice P. Bishop Museum in Honolulu from 1980 to 1990, serving concurrently as assistant director for research from 1985 to 1990. He has also served with the Smithsonian Institution's Flora of Ceylon Project. He was a post-doctoral Research Fellow at the Smithsonian; Staff Associate in charge of the Tropical Biology Initiative at the National Science Foundation, and as forest botanist with the (then) Office of Forests, Department of Primary Industry, Papua New Guinea. He has published or edited over seventy articles and books. Dr. Sohmer has had wide fieldwork experience in Philippine tropical forests.

BEN WALLACE (Ph.D. in anthropology, University of Wisconsin) is Professor of Anthropology, Assistant Provost, and Director of the International Office at Southern Methodist University. While his earlier research was devoted to the ecology of marginal slash-and-burn farmers, his more recent research has been directed toward designing strategies to help rural peoples reclaim their denuded environment. His publications include *Good Roots: Ugat ng Buhay: Helping Farmers Reclaim Their Environment; The Invisible Resource: Women's Work in Bangladesh; Contemporary Pacific Societies* (edited with Victoria Lockwood and Thomas Harding); and *Hill and Valley Farmers: Socio-Economic Change among a Philippine People.*

Introduction

The chapters in this small volume were first presented at a symposium in Dallas, Texas, on Sunday and Monday, September 24–25, 2000. The symposium title was the same as the title of the present volume, "What Place For Hunter-Gatherers in Millennium Three?" The symposium began in Dallas with a Sunday evening reception and Filipino banquet followed by a discussion period. On Monday, the daytime session was held at SIL's International Linguistics Center, and the evening session in the Hughes-Triggs Auditorium at Southern Methodist University.

The symposium was cosponsored by the Department of Anthropology at SMU and SIL International. The speakers included seven internationally known scholars (six anthropologists and one tropical forest ecologist). These were Drs. Robert Bailey (University of Illinois at Chicago), Bion Griffin (University of Hawai'i), Thomas Headland (SIL), Robert Hitchcock (University of Nebraska), Navin K. Rai (senior social development specialist with the World Bank), S. H. ("Sy") Sohmer (president of the Botanical Research Institute of Texas), and Ben Wallace (Southern Methodist University). The symposium was the second part of a three-part lecture series organized for the year 2000 by the International Museum of Cultures, in Dallas. This was in conjunction with the IMC's new Philippine Agta Exhibit (http://www.sil.org/imc/agta.htm). This exhibit explored profound environmental changes, completely beyond Agta control, that have thrust them into a period of rapid and irreversible cultural and social change. Reviews considered it a "must see" for everyone interested in the changing social environment of the remaining hunter-gatherer societies in our world today. (See photographs of the Exhibit on pp. xxii–xxiii.)

The seven speakers picked up on the IMC exhibit theme, but took it beyond just the Agta and just the Philippines. Five of the speakers are experts in hunting and gathering societies, or what may be better referred to as "Post-Foraging Societies" as we enter the third millennium today. The other two speakers are specialists on tropical forests. Three of the speakers (Griffin, Headland, and Rai) spoke first on the Agta. Then Sy Sohmer, a specialist on Philippine tropical forests, described the devastating deforestation in the Philippines since the 1960s, and Ben Wallace told about his reforestation projects in northwestern Luzon. Bob Bailey and Bob Hitchcock then took the audience beyond the Philippines. Bailey described the same problems as the Agta have, but for the Central African Pygmies where he works. Then Hitchcock did the same for the San Bushmen post-foragers where he works in southern Africa. All of the speakers wove the problems of indigenous human rights into their presentations.

Only six of the original seven presentations are published here. Unfortunately, Navin Rai was unable to get his paper to us in time for inclusion in this volume. We hope that Rai will submit his essay to us later. Rai has conducted years of scholarly work in the Philippines. He lived with the Agta for fifteen months in 1979–1980, and worked for five years in 1995–1999, helping the Agta to successfully secure ancestral domain claims for their lands in Quirino Province. We hope to see his perspective on the future of the Agta published soon.

In the first chapter of this volume, Hitchcock opens with a discussion of the changes that occurred during the twentieth century among the San Bushmen people of the Kalahari Desert in Africa. The San are the most extensively studied of any foraging societies on earth, and Hitchcock has been studying them for over two decades. He focuses in his present essay on the human rights issues among the San and their unique problems as they struggle with technological and political development at the dawn of the twenty-first century and the third millennium.

In the second essay, Bailey addresses the theme of this volume: what is in store for the future of today's remaining hunter-gatherer societies? What place is there for foraging peoples as they enter the new millennium? He draws upon his two decades of research among Pygmy foragers in Central Africa as he attempts to answer this question.

With chapter three, we move to the Philippines. But before we look at the Agta peoples there, Wallace first introduces us in his essay to the huge problems of tropical deforestation in that nation of 7,100 islands. Wallace is one of the few scholars to have implemented a successful reforestation project in the Philippines, or anywhere in the tropical world, for that matter. It was for that reason that we asked him to participate in our September 2000 symposium, and why we asked him to describe here what we consider one of the few successful applied anthropology reforestation projects in the tropical world. Since the Philippine forests have been almost completely destroyed in the last half-century, this small project will prove encouraging news to environmentalists and others. Why has this development project succeeded when so many such endeavors end in failure? This essay provides an answer to that question.

In the fourth chapter, Headland introduces readers to Southeast Asia's Negrito peoples in general, and then to the several Agta ethnolinguistic populations in particular. In both cases he reviews the drastic depopulation of these Negrito groups during the twentieth century—including Negrito populations in the Malay Peninsula and the Andaman Islands, as well as the Philippines—most of them to the point of extinction. His essay outlines the reasons for the depopulation of these foraging societies. Drawing from his own fieldwork among the Philippine Agta, Headland illustrates the problem with Agta case studies. He focuses here on three main causes for the problem: the recent destruction of the Negritos' forest homelands, imposed "development" programs by outsiders, and especially violations of indigenous human rights and land rights.

In the fifth essay to this volume, Griffin describes the long trajectory of change among the Agta groups with whom he has lived at various times beginning in 1972. He describes three main periods of Agta history: from 20,000 years ago up to the eve of European arrival in the 1500s, then from the Spanish period up to the end of the second millennium (1999). Then he suggests how the Agta peoples may change as they enter the third millennium. The Agta showed an amazing ability to adapt to their changing world around them during the historical period (1500–1999). While Griffin sees the Agta future as bleak, he holds some optimism that even though their traditional culture and languages may vanish in the twenty-first century, there is hope that they can continue to adapt to the greater changes to come.

In the sixth chapter, Sohmer describes aspects of his botanical research in Philippine tropical forests. He defines the term "forest" from his particular perspective and describes how lay people and anthropologists have so often failed to understand what a forest really is from a biological/ecological perspective. They have often, as he states, failed to see the "forest for the trees." As he argues persuasively, a forest is much more than the trees. He brings his readers to understand the main message of his argument, that the Philippines, once 96% forest, and estimated to be 30% old-growth forest in the 1930s, today probably has only about 3% of its old-growth forest remaining. His chapter thus underscores the message of this volume, the question of what will happen to Philippine Negrito foragers now, in this third millennium, with all their forest and its resources gone.

In the seventh chapter, Headland highlights the theme of this volume by illustrating with photographs how the Sierra Madre rainforest has changed—and with it the Agta culture—during the forty years he has been doing fieldwork in eastern Luzon.

The final chapter is a long bibliography review of 174 references of documents on the Agta peoples that would be of interest to scholars.

It goes without saying that the arguments of the authors of these chapters are their own, and not necessarily the consensus of everyone on the original panel at SMU where these papers were first presented.

Following the seven main chapters in the book, we close with two reviews. The first is a reprint of a critical museum review of the IMC's Agta museum exhibit that was originally published in the June 2001 issue of *American Anthropologist*. The second review is a newspaper report by Katie Menzer of the Agta exhibit that was published in the *The Dallas Morning News* on May 7, 2000.

Thomas N. Headland

Doris E. Blood

The Agta Exhibit, at the International Museum of Cultures in Dallas, centered on this manikin of an Agta man making fire by friction.

Tom Headland kneeling beside manikin of Agta man in his lean-to shelter making fire by friction.

Tom Headland shares a laugh with Museum Director Bill Merrifield. Between them in the background is the manikin of the Agta making fire. Behind the lean-to is a large photomural of the ocean of Casiguran Bay with a rising hill in the background. The hill was recently deforested and denuded by several small landslides. (This ocean-hillside photo was taken by John Early while visiting the Casiguran Agta area with Headland in 1994.)

A glass case in the Agta Exhibit; it displays some of the many types of Agta arrows. The large color photographs on the wall are of Agta people and scenes of their now-deforested homelands.

Chapter 1

Human Rights, Development, and the San of Southern Africa

Robert K. Hitchcock

The San (Bushmen, Basarwa) of the Kalahari Desert and adjacent areas of southern Africa are people who, like many other indigenous and minority peoples, are deeply committed to promoting and institutionalizing their socio-economic, political, civil, and cultural rights. Known to the public as some of the last representatives of African hunter-gatherer peoples, the San today pursue mixed economic systems, live in well-established villages, and participate extensively in the regional and world economy. Numbering some 88,000 in six southern Africa countries (Angola, Botswana, Namibia, South Africa, Zambia, and Zimbabwe), the contemporary San are some of the most active indigenous peoples in Africa in terms of efforts to promote human rights and sustainable community-based development.

Human Rights and the San

The human rights issues with which the San have to deal generally are similar to those of indigenous peoples in other parts of the world, although the San do have to face pressures that are somewhat unique. Discrimination against them has been a pervasive problem. The San have long faced difficulties in getting access to land and natural resources. They often are the last hired and the first fired in employment situations. San tend to get harsher treatment before the courts, and in the past they did not have the right to represent themselves or even to speak in court hearings. Their subsistence rights have been infringed upon by wildlife laws that made it illegal for them to hunt many of the species of game upon which they depended for food, materials, and income.

Substantial numbers of San have been deprived of their land, much of which was given to other groups or taken over by the state. The government subjected them to resettlement programs in which they were required to leave their ancestral areas and to move to new places that had been set aside for them. In these places, San all too frequently experience unemployment or underemployment. The areas generally are too small to allow residents to continue to forage for a living. In many cases they are located far from places where wild plant resources

1

exist in abundance so people have to expend considerable time and energy to obtain even minimal wild resources. As a result, residents of settlements often have low incomes, and they experience nutritional stress even in those cases where government or relief agencies have provided food and other goods.

Like many peoples in southern Africa and elsewhere in the world, the San face major constraints in getting access to resources, funding, and development assistance. A list of some of the human rights challenges facing the San is presented in appendix 1.

Traditionally, the San were hunter-gatherers and agropastoralists who lived in small groups of twenty-five to fifty people who were tied together through bonds of kinship, marriage, friendship, and reciprocity. These groups moved about the landscape, aggregating and dispersing according to season, resource availability, and the distribution of other groups. Some San groups exploited as many as 150 species of wild plants and over forty species of wild animals. San women provided the bulk of the diet through their plant collecting activities, while men contributed protein through hunting, fishing, and collecting. The generalized subsistence system of the San meant that they did not place too much pressure on any one resource, and they were able to buffer themselves against scarcity by relying on other resources if their target species declined.

The San generally were relatively successful in coping with environmental uncertainty. This was in part because of their vast environmental knowledge, their information sharing-systems, their technology, and the fact that their population densities generally were low, so they did not put too much pressure on resources. The landscape in which the San reside and earn their living is divided into tracts that comprise the basic subsistence and residential areas of local groups. Some of the territories of the San contained rock art, both pictographs (rock paintings) and petroglyphs (rock engravings). This art may be related to traditional San healing and rainmaking practices, according to some analysts. The art may also serve an information communication function, letting people know of the socially and ideologically significant status of the place.

The San and the Political Process

In the past, San in various parts of southern Africa did not have rights to participate in the political process that was recognized officially. In Botswana, for example, San were considered *bolata* 'serfs', and they did not have the same rights as other people. Until the end of the nineteenth century, they lacked property rights, and they could not even arrange their own marriages in areas where other groups were present.

In Botswana, San have participated in political activities since the time of independence in September 1966. In Namibia and South Africa, substantial numbers of San voted in the elections that took place after the end of *apartheid.* In Ghanzi District, Botswana, which has a population made up of a large proportion (43%) of San, three San were elected to positions on the District Council in 1989 and seven in 1994. In the October 1999 Botswana elections, a female San leader from Chobe District was elected to the House of Chiefs as a subchief. San have continued to press Southern African governments for recognition of their leaders. In Namibia, the government has recognized two traditional authorities, one in Nyae Nyae (Ju/'hoansi) and the other in Tsumkwe District West (former West Bushmanland) (!Kung, Khwe, and Vasekele San).

Major events in the history of San politics in the 1990s include the holding of regional conferences on San peoples, one in Windhoek, Namibia in June 1992 and another in Gaborone, Botswana in October 1993. At these meetings the governments of southern Africa went on record to say that they were committed to helping San and other people in remote areas. San spokespersons noted at these conferences that they wanted access to education, health, social services, jobs, land, and development assistance. In general, San said that they wanted the rights of political participation and protection of cultural rights as well as the opportunity to have a say in matters relating to their own economic, social, cultural, and spiritual development.

The San have engaged in many debates about their goals and objectives. Virtually all San would like a greater say in decisions that affect them, and they would all like to see their standards of living enhanced. The San have expressed their desires: (1) that they be allowed to participate fully in needs assessments, development planning, and project implementation; (2) that they be provided information on which to base decisions; (3) that they have secure rights to land and natural resources; and (4) that they be allowed the right to determine their own futures. Like other indigenous peoples, San want the right to practice their own cultural traditions and to teach their children mother tongue languages. The San also maintain that they wish to ensure their security rights, those rights related to the security of the person, including the right to be free from torture, mistreatment, and execution without trial.

Social and Cultural Rights among San

Various San organizations and their supporters have made efforts to promote human rights and implement innovative community-based development strategies. They have built capacity for local decision-making in a number of ways. They have held workshops or community discussion sessions in which ideas about development were addressed. They have also promoted hands-on training of various kinds. They have utilized nonformal educational strategies and innovative learner-centered techniques, including engaging in problem-solving exercises, group discussions, use of relevant case examples, and doing role plays about situations in which communities and individuals sometimes find themselves. San have also advocated for their rights at the local, national, regional, and international levels.

The San have a deep and heartfelt commitment to maintaining traditional cultural values and belief systems. Many San have sought to enhance their culture through the active promotion of traditional activities (arts, crafts, dance) and the learning and teaching of mother tongue San languages. In the case of language education, the Village Schools Project associated with the Nyae Nyae Development Foundation and the Namibian Ministry of Basic Education and Culture has enabled Ju/'hoansi children to learn the Ju/'hoan language. Kuru Development Trust and their coworkers are promoting similar linguistic and literacy efforts in the Nharo San language in western Botswana.

Many San are seeking to retain and promote indigenous cultural and environmental knowledge. San in some areas demonstrate to visitors various ways in which wild plant foods and medicines are found, prepared, and utilized. Others take safari hunters out with them as they use traditional weapons. While being cautious about the kinds of stereotypic notions outsiders sometimes possess, the San strive to be seen as people who are sophisticated both in a cultural and an ethical sense and who manage resources responsibly.

Successful development and effective management of human and natural resources imply the formation of viable institutional partnerships between the state, the private sector, and local communities. Thus far, at least ten community trusts in which San are involved have been established in southern Africa. The San have made efforts to ensure that these institutions will be both representative and accountable.

In one case, the Ju/'hoansi San and Mbanderu (Herero) of /Xai/Xai, a village of some 380 people in western Ngamiland, Botswana, established a community trust, the /Xai/Xai Tlhabololo Trust in October 1997. In 2000, it was estimated that members of the trust would receive over 250,000 Pula from a safari company for the rights to operate in their area (a Pula is worth about U.S. $0.17). The local people reserved some of the quota for their own purposes, maintaining a portion of it for subsistence and another portion as a reserve for the future. Over twenty people now have regular employment, and food, medicines, and other goods are available to the /Xai/Xai trust members.

San communities continue work to prevent forced relocation and land dispossession, loss of subsistence hunting rights, and the erosion of culture, often in collaboration with a committed network of San nongovernmental organizations and support organizations. For example, First People of the Kalahari (FPK) is a Botswana-based San nongovernmental organization founded in 1993 that has sought to promote the land and resource rights of the San and Bakgalagadi out of the Central Kalahari Game Reserve, Africa's second largest conservation area. First People of the Kalahari and two international indigenous peoples support groups, International Work Group for Indigenous Affairs and Survival International, expressed their concerns about the treatment of people who are engaged in subsistence hunting. They have provided information to local people on land and resource rights. In the late 1990s, First People of the Kalahari expanded its operations to include mapping of traditional territories using Geographic Positioning Systems (GPS) instruments and the making of maps of ancestral territories in anticipation of a land claim, and it trained local people in natural resource management and community development. Unfortunately, the land claim effort was unsuccessful, with a case against the Government of Botswana being dismissed by the High Court in Botswana in April 2002.

Kuru Development Trust, an indigenous multipurpose San development organization established in 1986, has assisted the San in their struggles to promote development and empowerment. Kuru is committed to the development of the San and other marginalized rural minorities who live in western Botswana. In addition to its work in capacity building and community economic development activities, Kuru is involved in the mapping of San traditional territories in the Dobe area in western Botswana and along the Okavango River and western side of the Okavango Delta. Kuru undertook these projects because it realizes that documentation of oral histories, demarcation of traditional territories through land mapping, and provision of communities with their own documented histories are an important tool for empowerment, awareness, and potential negotiations concerning rights and access to land.

In some cases San have been able to obtain access to freehold (i.e., private) land. This was the case, for example, with Dqae Qare Game Farm in Ghanzi District, a conservation and game management project that Kuru undertook several years ago. At Dqae Qare, tourists are able to stay in a fine old Afrikaaner farmhouse managed by San. The tourists can take guided bush walks to see wildlife and learn how local San track animals and find wild plants. An important part of the program is the development of basic business skills such as bookkeeping, community awareness, and marketing.

In South Africa, San communities are making progress in their efforts to obtain rights to land and to compensation for resources lost in the past. In the 1990s, the /Khomani San of South Africa made a formal claim for the area in and around the Kalahari Gemsbok Park in South Africa under South Africa's *Restitution of Land Rights Act* of 1994. Eventually, the case was settled out of court, and the /Khomani received some 25,000 hectares of land outside the national park. They also got the right to co-manage land and tourism in the national park itself. In addition, the /Khomani are receiving cash compensation for loss of their lands and resources. In 1999, The Kalahari Gemsbok Park became the first transfrontier national park in southern Africa, with Botswana and South Africa sharing responsibility for management. What is unique about this transboundary park is the degree to which local people now play a role in decision-making about its future.

Conclusions

Clearly, San are engaging in activities to promote networking and are seeking to establish regional and national support organizations. The Working Group of Indigenous Minorities in southern Africa (WIMSA) was founded in January 1996 at the request of the San of Botswana, Namibia, and South Africa. WIMSA serves as a lobbying and advocacy organization that seeks to promote the rights of San.

WIMSA staff members undertake a variety of activities ranging from training to coordinating work among San and other communities and organizations. They inform the public about issues of concern to San.

In many ways, the growth of WIMSA, the San nongovernment organizations such as Kuru and First People of the Kalahari, and the various San community-based organizations represents what can be viewed as a kind of social and political movement among San people. This movement aims to promote the civil, political, and socioeconomic rights of African indigenous peoples who are minorities in the states in which they reside. A major strategy that is being employed by the San is to ensure that the cultural identities of San peoples are not only recognized but also that members of San groups take great pride in them. Another major strategy has been to negotiate with the state over issues such as land rights and recognition of local leaders. While not all of their strategies have been successful, the San have learned important lessons, and they have been able, in some cases, to enhance their living standards, raise public awareness of their situations, and increase the control that they have over portions of southern Africa. Progress that they make in these and other areas can and will serve as models for indigenous and other peoples elsewhere in Africa and the world.

Appendix 1: Current human rights challenges faced by the Kalahari San

Land Rights, Water Rights, and Resource Rights
- Landlessness and lack of ability to get land or to retain it (tenure insecurity)
- Involuntary removal from parks, reserves, national monuments, and other categories of conservation land
- Conflicts over access rights to certain areas of land in communal (tribal) zones
- Reduction of subsistence hunting due to restriction on access to licenses

- Frequent arrests, detentions, and sometimes mistreatment of individuals suspected of violating hunting laws
- Restriction of access to ostriches and ostrich eggshell products, which reduces income of families and particularly women
- Restriction on access to wild plants, both medicinal and food plants, due to commercialization and licensing activities
- Difficulty in getting access to water in some areas and failure to provide water in a timely fashion

Economic Rights
- Limited access to food in some areas, notably on cattle posts, ranches, and in and around conservation areas such as the Central Kalahari Game Reserve
- High percentages of people living below the Poverty Datum Line (PDL)
- Low employment, few jobs, and low wages
- Relatively high prices that have to be paid in remote rural areas

Social, Cultural, and Language Rights
- Lack of recognition of the San as a tribe (political representation issues)
- Local San leaders are often not recognized, or, if they do get official leadership positions, their authority is not always recognized
- Lack of ability to get teaching done in mother tongue languages
- In terms of education, San children are sometimes treated poorly in schools

Justice Issues, Conflict, and Refugees
- Tend to receive harsher sentences if they are convicted of crimes than other groups
- Forced to flee warfare and conflict situations, such as those in Angola and the Caprivi Region of Namibia, and take refuge in neighboring countries, notably Botswana

Health and Physical Well-being
- Low to moderate health status of many San
- Rising problems of disease, including HIV/AIDs, tuberculosis, diabetes, and heart disease
- Poor nutrition among San in some areas
- Food relief and destitute payments creating dependency

Some References on the San

Barnard, Alan. 1992. *Hunters and Herders of Southern Africa: A Comparative Ethnography of the Khoisan Peoples.* Cambridge: Cambridge University Press.

Biesele, Megan, and Kxao Royal. 1997. *San.* New York: The Rosen Publishing Group.

Biesele, Megan, and Paul Weinberg. 1990. *Shaken Roots: The Bushmen of Namibia.* Marshalltown, South Africa: EDA Publications.

Gordon, Robert J., and Stuart Sholto Douglas. 2000. *The Bushman Myth: The Making of a Namibian Underclass.* 2nd edition. Boulder and London: Westview Press.

Hitchcock, Robert K. 1996. *Kalahari Communities: Bushmen and the Politics of the Environment in Southern Africa.* Copenhagen, Denmark: International Work Group for Indigenous Affairs.

Katz, Richard, Megan Biesele, and Verna St. Denis. 1997. *Healing Makes Our Hearts Happy: Spirituality and Cultural Transformation among the Kalahari Ju/'hoansi.* Rochester, Vt: Inner Traditions.

Lee, Richard B., and Richard Daly. 1999. *The Cambridge Encyclopedia of Hunters and Gatherers.* Cambridge: Cambridge University Press.

Saugestad, Sidsel. 2001. *The Inconvenient Indigenous: Remote Area Development in Botswana, Donor Assistance, and the First People of the Kalahari.* Stockholm: The Nordic Africa Institute.

Schweitzer, Peter R., Megan Biesele, and Robert K. Hitchcock. 2000. *Hunters and Gatherers in the Modern World: Conflict, Resistance and Self-Determination.* New York and Oxford: Berghahn Books.

Smith, Andy, Candy Malherbe, Mat Guenther, and Penny Berens. 2000. *The Bushmen of Southern Africa: A Foraging Society in Transition.* Cape Town: David Philip Publishers, and Athens: Ohio University Press.

Suzman, James, ed. 2001. *An Introduction to the Regional Assessment of the Status of the San in Southern Africa.* Windhoek, Namibia: Legal Assistance Center.

Widlok, Thomas. 1999. *Living on Mangetti: 'Bushman' Autonomy and Namibian Independence.* Oxford: Oxford University Press.

Web sites on the San

http://www.kalaharipeoples.org/
http://www.san.org.za/
http://www.firstpeoples.org

Chapter 2

The Efe Foragers in the Ituri Forest, Democratic Republic of Congo: Survival in the New Millennium?

Robert C. Bailey

This essay attempts to address the theme of the present volume: What is in store for the future of today's remaining hunter-gatherer societies? What place is there for these foraging peoples as they, with the rest of us, enter the new millennium?

Background

Approximately 200 million hectares of forest lie within the boundaries of six countries in central Africa. This area of forest represents 20% of the world's tropical moist forest, second in size only to Amazonia, and contains a wide variety of flora, fauna, and human cultures. The majority of people living in the region rely upon the resources of the forest for a significant proportion of their subsistence. Outside of the few cities and towns in the forest, the predominant mode of subsistence is slash-and-burn horticulture. In addition, there are still populations that make their living by hunting forest animals and collecting plant materials. These people, whom we refer to as foragers, consume hunted and gathered forest resources themselves, and they trade them to farmers in exchange for agricultural produce. This report briefly describes one particular group of farmers, the Lese, and one group of foragers, the Efe, who together subsist in the northern Ituri Forest on the northeast lip of the Congo River Basin. It also discusses some of the challenges these people face as modernization and demographic change sweep over central Africa.

The Ituri forest lies on the northeastern lip of the Congo River Basin at an altitude between 700–1,000 meters. This area contains the largest number and greatest biomass of faunal species of any forested area of comparable size in Africa, and 15% of the species are endemic. The Ituri is bounded on the north and northeast by savanna and in the east by the rich highlands formed by the uplifting and volcanization associated with the western rift valley. It is contiguous to the lowland forest to the south and west where the rivers drain into the Congo River. The southern portion of the Ituri Forest, which extends to the equator, is gently undulating, but to the north in the area where we have done our studies, there are frequent outcroppings of smooth, basal granite rising several hundred feet above the forest. The climax vegetation in the Ituri is characterized by three dominant species of tall, hardwood legumes in the sub-family Caesalpineaceae. In the south and west, *Gilbertiodendron* dominates to such an extent that it can constitute 90% of the standing vegetation. But in the north, where we have been working with the Efe and the Lese, mixed species stands of *Cynometra alexandrii* and *Brachystegia laurentii* dominate the mature forest vegetation with a number of other tall species interspersed between these codominants.

The Lese Farmers

Within the Ituri forest there are two kinds of people subsisting in two different, but overlapping and interdependent ways. One group is the slash-and-burn horticulturists known as the Lese. The Lese live in small villages numbering from fifteen to 125 inhabitants. Residence is mainly viripatrilocal (men stay in a circumscribed area with their male relatives for most of their lives, while women marry out of their native villages) so that within any one village all the men are related to one another and women tend not to be related to each other. Wives were once obtained principally through sister exchange but now payment of bride wealth is the preferred method of marriage. Within the study area 21% of Lese men are married polygynously and the maximum number of wives married to one man is four.

Within a mile or so of the village, the Lese clear patches of mature and late successional forest, usually a quarter to half an acre per year per family. They cultivate primarily cassava and bananas for subsistence and peanuts and rice as sporadic cash crops. These cash crops and small amounts of coffee are sold to the few merchants who are willing to expose their vehicles to the treacherous conditions of the road. Average annual income per Lese household is less than $50 U.S. In addition to cassava and bananas as the main subsistence sources of carbohydrates, the Lese also cultivate sweet potato, corn, squash, beans, sesame, and occasionally taro and yams. For their gardens, they clear forest towards the end of the rainy season in November and December, so that during the dry season—December through February—the area of vegetation that is felled is allowed to dry. Then, at the end of the dry season during late February or March they torch the dry vegetation and it burns, putting ashes back into the soil. They typically plant their crops in late March and early April.

Once gardens are cleared, women do most of the labor of planting, weeding, harvesting, and processing the crops, but they by no means do all of that labor. Their primary source of fat is oil from the palm *Elaeis guineensis,* which is cooked with the leaves of cassava to produce a staple called *sombe.* Meat and fish are also cooked with palm oil. Although fishing in the small streams around the villages is a frequent and favorite activity of Lese women, fish do not account for a significant proportion of their diet. Most Lese own a few chickens, but only four households out of approximately 200 own goats and none own pigs.

The Efe Foragers

Living in association with the Lese horticulturists, are a group of seminomadic hunting and gathering people who call themselves Efe. In Western terms we refer to them as pygmies, but this is considered a pejorative term by the Efe themselves. There are currently four populations of so-called pygmies, collectively called the Bambuti, living in the Ituri forest. They are not separate populations in a demographic sense as they are continuously distributed geographically and they intermarry, but they are differentiated by language, by custom, and by technology. Probably the best known of these groups is the Mbuti, made famous primarily by Colin Turnbull through his book, *The Forest People* (Turnbull 1961). The Mbuti hunt primarily with nets and they associate themselves with Bantu-speaking farmers, called the Babila. The Efe, with whom we are concerned here, are known as archers or bow hunters. They have the broadest distribution of all the Bambuti extending over most of the northern Ituri down to the southeast near Beni, and in most of this range, they associate themselves with various subgroups of the Sudanic-speaking Lese.

The Efe live in small temporary encampments with three to fifty residents. The size and composition of camps is very flexible, with divisions occurring at the level of the household. However, residence is primarily viripatrilocal and most camps are composed of loose patriclans. For example, censuses from eighteen Efe camps showed 83% of men residing in their patriclan and 87% of married women residing with their husband's patriclan (Bailey and Aunger 1989). The Efe identify themselves by patriclan and can trace their ancestry back two to four generations, identifying each forbear, male or female, by patriclan. Marriage is forbidden within the patriclan of either the mother or father. Ideally, marriage is by sister exchange but only 40% of Efe men are able to achieve this ideal, which makes disputes over marriage and children frequent, and in many cases disputes endure for generations. Bridewealth is absent and bride service is very brief when it occurs at all.

For approximately seven months during the year, Efe reside in temporary camps that are situated near the Lese villages, often on the edge of the forest near an active or recently abandoned garden. During the other five months, Efe camp deeper in the forest, but never in my experience more than an eight-hour walk from a village. When they are living in the forest, Efe move camp approximately every two weeks. Actual campsites are changed less frequently when they are near the villages, but the number and composition of individuals at any one site is more variable because individual households tend to change residents more often.

Throughout the year, Efe gain their subsistence from both forest resources and cultivated foods. The great majority of Efe do not cultivate crops themselves and none that I studied had gardens at any time during my research. They hunt and gather forest resources for their own consumption and for exchange with villagers. Meat, honey, a few gathered fruits and nuts, and building materials are brought from the forest to the villages to exchange for cultivated foods, tobacco, cannabis, and material goods, primarily cloth and iron implements. Efe also provide labor to Lese and receive food and goods in return, usually on the same day.

Efe women supply most of the labor in assisting villager women in their many tasks related to food production and processing. On a typical day in an Efe village camp, the majority of the Efe women will spend at least a portion of their day in the villagers' gardens, and in a forest camp at least a few of the women will go to the village. Those that remain behind might fish or gather some forest foods and take care of children left behind by busy mothers.

Efe men, on the other hand, work for villagers infrequently—primarily to help Lese men clear their gardens—and spend most of their time in subsistence-related activities in the forest. Hunting and honey collection are almost exclusively male activities, while gathering is done by both sexes. Men hunt alone or in cooperative groups ranging in size from four to twenty-seven men. Their most frequent prey are six species of duikers (*Cephalophus* spp.), the water chevrotain, and monkeys. Besides hunting, finding and collecting honey is an important male activity. Men most often find beehives when they are alone in the forest, but they generally wait until a later time to extract the honey with a small number of other men (Bailey 1991).

Challenges to Efe Survival—the Demographic Challenge

There are two salient challenges that Efe face. I would classify these as challenges to their culture and demographic challenges. With regard to the demographic challenges, first refer to figure 2.1, which is the distribution of live births among postmenopausal Efe women interviewed in 1981. As figure 2.1 shows, approximately 28% or twenty-five out of eighty-nine postmenopausal women had no live births at all, and another sixteen out of eighty-nine women (18%) had just one live birth. These high rates of primary and secondary infertility are occurring in a population that uses no Western contraception and in which there is high value placed on children and women who have many children. In other words, most women are trying to have as many children as possible.

Looking at table 2.1, we see that the reproductive histories of these eighty-nine postmenopausal Efe women translate into an average number of live births per women of just 2.56 births. Then, looking at the mortality rates, one can see that infant mortality (that is mortality in the first year of life) is 14%, and that 17.5% of children die before the age of five. Given this low level of fertility, combined with a relatively high level of mortality, this is a declining population. What causes this low level of fertility? The answer is sexually transmitted diseases, particularly gonorrhea and chlamydia. These cause tubal scarring and eventually occlusions in women and result in high levels of infertility (Bailey and Aunger 1995). Sexually transmitted diseases, then, pose a significant threat to the demographic survival of the Efe. This threat has likely been true since the 1880s with the advent of Arab ivory and slave traders and somewhat later with forced labor and disruption of traditional family structures in the early 1900s by Belgian colonialists.

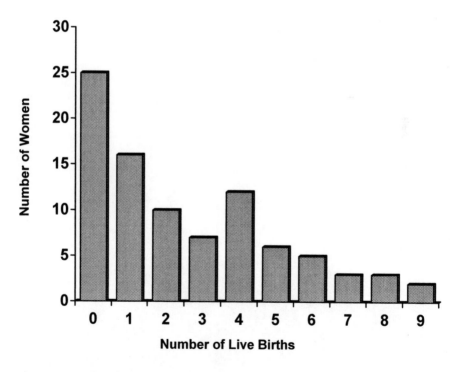

Figure 2.1. The distribution of 228 live births by 89 postmenopausal Efe women. The mean number of live births per woman is 2.56, and 28% of women have no live births.

Table 2.1. Results from reproductive histories of 89 postmenopausal women
showing the mean number of live births per woman and the cumulative
proportion of childhood mortality by age class (Bailey and Aunger 1995)

Live Births		Deaths by Age Class			
Male	Female	0–1	0–4	0–9	0–14
119	109	32	40	48	51
	2.56	.140	.175	.211	.224

In addition to a high incidence of STDs causing infertility, another threat to the
demographic survival of the Efe is dramatic fluctuations in fertility rates caused
by high workloads and periodic poor energy balance. Even those women who
are fertile experience periods of anovulatory menstrual cycles.
Figure 2.2 shows the pattern of monthly rainfall in the Ituri forest. These data
were collected over a nine-year period in the 1980s. One sees here the pro-
nounced dry season in December, January, and February. This is a fairly regular
pattern. However, there are years in which this seasonal pattern of rainfall is dis-
rupted. Such uncertainty in rainfall in turn causes uncertainty in the agricultural
cycle. My colleagues and I have shown in previously published studies that disruptions in rainfall cause disruptions in garden size in the Lese. That situation
then causes disruptions in the food supply, which cause dramatic fluctuations in
energy balance among the Lese and to a lesser extent among the Efe (Bailey et
al. 1992).

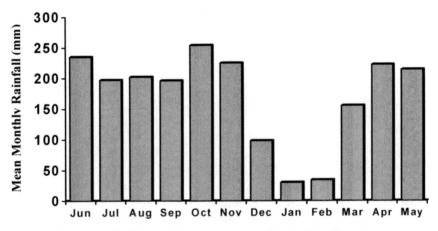

Figure 2.2. Mean monthly rainfall (mm) measured at the Ngodingodi
Research Station, Ituri Region, Democratic Republic of Congo, March
1980–December 1987, showing the dry season in December–February.

Further, Ellison and colleagues have shown that these fluctuations in energy balance cause changes in ovulatory frequencies in women (Ellison, Peacock, and Lager 1989). In those seasons when women lose a significant amount of weight, there is also a significant reduction in ovulatory frequency. This, in turn, causes dramatic seasonality in birth. During the lean months, women are less likely to ovulate, and so the probability of conception is reduced. During months of plenty (with some lag time to recover from the lean periods), ovulatory frequency increases, and so chances of conception also rise (Bailey et al. 1992). The resulting seasonality in monthly conceptions adversely affects overall fertility, exacerbating the adverse affects of infertility due to STDs.

Therefore, the two challenges that the Lese and Efe face demographically are, first, low fertility rates caused by infertility due to high prevalence of sexually transmitted diseases, and, second, reduced fertility due to fluctuations in energy balance causing anovulatory menstrual cycles and subfecundity.

Challenges to Efe Cultural Survival

The Efe also face challenges to their cultural survival by virtue of the depletion of the Ituri forest by an onslaught of immigrants from other groups into the forest. These immigrants are attracted to the forest for its large areas of uncultivated land. The highlands to the east harbor some of the highest population densities in all of Africa. There is tremendous pressure on the land in these highlands, and people in those areas are now flooding down the western slope of the highlands into the Ituri. They come seeking available forest areas to clear and to grow crops, which they consume themselves. But they also clear large areas of forest for commercial agriculture. They transport their harvest in small trucks up to the highlands where they can fetch higher prices than they could in the forest. In addition to being more commercially minded, these immigrants tend to be better educated, more aggressive, and understand more about the politics of the region. The laws of the Congo are such that the Efe and the Lese do not have rights to their traditional lands so it is not difficult for immigrants to come into the area and for very little money, if any at all, lay claim to a patch of forest. In this way, immigrants essentially take ownership of the traditional lands of the Efe and Lese and exploit those lands for their own ends with no regard to conservation.

The government of the Democratic Republic of Congo has taken several steps to try to minimize the effects of immigrants coming into the forest. One very large and promising step has been for the government to declare a forest reserve, called the Okopi National Wildlife Refuge. Donor money has been put into the formation and maintenance of this reserve. Activities within the reserve are restricted, and now people are not permitted to clear forest or to extract timber or gold. The Efe and Lese are permitted access to the forest in limited ways, but in ways that, at least for the next several decades, probably will not change their lifestyle substantially. The greatest value of this reserve for the Efe is the protection of a substantial portion of their traditional lands in the Ituri forest, allowing the flora and fauna to be conserved and allowing the Efe and the Lese to continue their traditional subsistence strategies. One unfortunate aspect of the creation of the reserve is that the Efe and Lese had limited say in the decisions, and they have little influence in the management of the reserve (Bailey 1996). As increasing pressure is put on the Ituri, empowering the indigenous populations to make decisions regarding the land they have inhabited and used successfully for many generations is likely to be an effective strategy for achieving long-term conservation goals. Hopefully, the Efe and Lese will some day achieve a voice with regard to how their land is used and how its resources are conserved.

The creation of the Ituri Forest Peoples Fund (IFPF) is another step that has been taken to increase the chances for Efe survival. (For information about the IFPF, go to http://www2.bc.edu/~morellig/IturiForestPeoplesFund/HTML/fundfaqs.htm.) IFPF is a small grassroots development project, founded in 1989 by the Efe and Lese, with assistance from myself, David Wilkie, Gilda Morelli, and many colleagues who have conducted research with the Efe and Lese over the last twenty years. The goals of the IFPF are to assist the Lese and the Efe in improving their health, preventing disease, and improving their chances for an education. For the last thirteen years or so, the IFPF has assisted the Lese and the Efe in training indigenous people as rural health-care workers. The people themselves have built a rural health facility, and the IPFP assists with the purchase and supply of frequently needed medications, such as malarial prophylaxis and antibiotics. Without the hard work of the local people and the assistance of the IFPF, these simple items and the knowledge provided by rural health workers would not be available, and many easily preventable illnesses would go untreated. In addition, the Efe and Lese have built schoolhouses where there were none previously. The IFPF has provided the salaries for six teachers, who teach approximately 130 students through grade six.

These few small programs were started after a long and difficult decision process, initiated and run by the local people. The local people designed the programs, and they run the programs. As outsiders, we simply assist with funding and occasionally provide the perspective of outsiders who have seen or read about events not accessible to indigenous forest populations. Over the years, we believe this small project has resulted in the reduction in incidence of STDs, in greater survivorship of children, and in the broader education of a new generation of Lese and Efe. We all hope that through their own efforts and the IFPF their chances of survival as a population and as a culture are improving. By being educated they will be better equipped to deal with the outside forces that are proving to be so aggressive in taking their land and threatening their way of life.

References Cited

Bailey, Robert C. 1991. *The Behavioral Ecology of Efe Pygmy Men in the Ituri Forest, Zaire.* Ann Arbor, Mich.: Anthropological Papers, Museum of Anthropology, University of Michigan.

Bailey, Robert C. 1996. Promoting Biodiversity and Empowering Local People in Central African Forests. In L. E. Sponsel, T. N. Headland, and R. C. Bailey (eds.), *Tropical Deforestation: The Human Dimension,* 316–341. New York: Columbia University Press.

Bailey, Robert C., and R. Aunger. 1989. Significance of Social Relationships of Efe Pygmy Men in the Ituri Forest, Zaire. *American Journal of Physical Anthropology* 78:495–507.

Bailey, Robert C., and R. Aunger. 1995. Sexuality, Infertility and Sexually Transmitted Disease among Farmers and Foragers in Central Africa. In P. R. Abramson and S. D. Pinkerton (eds.), *Sexual Nature: Sexual Culture,* 195–222. Chicago: University of Chicago Press.

Bailey, Robert C., M. Jenike, G. Ellison, G. Bentley, A. Harrigan, and N. Peacock. 1992. The Ecology of Birth Seasonality among Agriculturalists in Central Africa. *Journal of Biosocial Science* 24:393–412.

Ellison, P., N. R. Peacock, and K. Lager. 1989. Ecology and Ovarian Function among Lese Women of the Ituri Forest, Zaire. *American Journal of Physical Anthropology* 78:519–526.

Turnbull, Colin M. 1961. *The Forest People.* New York: Simon and Schuster.

Chapter 3

Helping Farmers Reclaim their Land: Sustainable Development and the Philippine Good Roots Project

Ben J. Wallace

As has been dramatically demonstrated in the other chapters in this volume, "indigenous peoples have been, and continue to be, noticeably affected by the loss of the forestlands in and around the areas in which they live." In areas of the developing world where farming is the mainstay of life, farm families constantly have to adjust to ever-changing ecological conditions. Unless mechanisms are developed to help these farm families make adjustment to changing environmental conditions, the many problems associated with migration to the urban centers and rural poverty will become even more acute. An attempt is being made in the Philippines to address the issue of reforestation, along with farm management, in hope of bringing some stability to the rural areas.

The purpose of this essay is to present a case for an interdisciplinary research and development project.[1] In order to maximize the accomplishments of team members and minimize costs, all parts of the project are perceived as functionally interrelated such that any component or activity (e.g., personnel, land, research activity, etc.) is multipurpose. A multipurpose tree is a tree that contributes in more than one way to the sustainability of an agroforestry system (Von Carlowitz 1984). In just such a way, multipurpose research, as used here, is research in which each activity contributes in more than one way to the sustainability and the attainment of the goals of the project. Research team members, constituting what may be called a Multipurpose Research Team (MPRT), function as partially interchangeable parts of the whole. They contribute in more than one way to the sustainability of research and development activities. An ongoing project on agroforestry research and development in the province of Ilocos Norte, Philippines, provides illustrative materials for discussion here.

---

[1]The heart of any interdisciplinary research and development project is the scientific and support staff. I will always be indebted to Marilyn U. Tolentino, Gemma Domile, Antonio Garvida, Manuelito Calventas, and Magel Leano for their untiring work, dedication, insight, and friendship through the years of Good Roots.

19

The Good Roots Project

A memorandum of agreement on agroforestry research and development was signed on Earth Day 1991, between Southern Methodist University (through the SMU Institute for the Study of Earth and Man), Caltex (Philippines) Inc., and the Philippine Department of Environment and Natural Resources (DENR). This research and development project is a pioneer action in the Philippines because it is the first example of industry, government, and the academic community pooling their resources and talents. Thus, they are directing those resources toward the amelioration of some of the environmental and social problems facing this predominantly rural country. Ben Wallace, the initiator and overall director of the project from Southern Methodist University, is responsible for the oversight of all scientific and development activity. He holds final authority in this arena. Caltex Philippines provides the funds for the project and has final responsibility on a pre-approved five-year budget. Finally, the Philippine DENR monitors the scientific activities of the project, provides technical advice, and serves as liaison with other government agencies. This project, technically entitled "Multipurpose Tree Species, Wood Use, and Farming Systems Research" is popularly known simply as "Good Roots–*Ugat ng Buhay.*" The project represents a five-year commitment on the part of SMU, Caltex Philippines, and the Philippine DENR.[2]

The primary goal of Good Roots is to facilitate research and development on multipurpose tree species (MPTS) within the context of the whole farm or farming system. Good Roots is not a forestry project where hundreds of hectares of denuded hill slopes are to be reclaimed through the planting of selected tree species. Large-scale reforestation projects such as these are best left to large government agencies where hundreds of laborers can be employed to plant seedlings.

The Good Roots project is carried out in four communities located in the northwestern-most province of the Philippines. One community practices slash-and-burn agriculture; one has a technology based on dry field cultivation; one practices wet paddy cultivation; and one uses all aspects of these agricultural technologies. In total, Good Roots serves 506 households or a population of almost 3,000 people and covers approximately 3,000 hectares, 482 of which are under cultivation. The swidden or slash-and-burn farmers in the study are members of the ethnic minority Apayao-Isneg, known locally as Yapayao. The other three communities are comprised of Ilocano speakers.

---

[2]The Good Roots I project was replicated (1997–2001) in the province of Batangas (Philippines) under the name Good Roots II. Caltex Philippines continues its support of the project.

The Multipurpose Experience

The problem, simply stated, became: how to do quality agroforestry research and development, benefiting a relatively large number of people, at a fraction of the cost often spent by international donor agencies. Instead of spending five, eight, twenty, or even forty million dollars over five years, a common practice by international standards, the budget would be limited to approximately one-half million dollars over five years. Instead of twenty, forty, or even more employees, there could be only four to six. There could be no office building or research stations, which would be too costly. Instead of numerous trucks there could be only one, and expatriate consultants would have to be severely limited. The challenge became how to control costs and create a Multipurpose Research Team to address the demands of multipurpose research and development within a Farming Systems Research and Development approach (CGIAR 1978; De Walt 1985; Norman et al. 1979; Jones and Wallace 1986; Rhoades 1985; Shaner et al. 1982), especially as related to Farming Systems Research and MPTS (Wallace 1989).[3]

The goals of the Good Roots project are accomplished through the efforts of a Multipurpose Research Team (MPRT) that is composed of five people: a male anthropologist, a male agriculturist, a male forester, a female social science specialist, and a female extension specialist. An adequate MPRT in the Philippines, as well as in many other parts of the world, should be comprised of both male and female researchers. Farming activity and related cultural beliefs are often gender-specific and are most efficiently addressed in like-gender situations. But even when the various farming tasks are conducted by both males and females, a mixed-gender team is the most effective because an interdisciplinary approach to farming involves an examination of farm families and all farmers: men, women, and children.

An expensive part of most international development projects is the cost of permanent scientific personnel and local and expatriate consultants. Good Roots project costs are reduced by employing a small scientific staff and keeping the only expatriate member of the team, the initiator and director, in the field for only three or four months a year.

The director of the project is an anthropologist with more than two decades of research and development experience in Southeast Asia. The other team members are Filipinos with considerable experience in research and development. While designing the Good Roots research and development activity, they decided that the goals of the project could best be attained with a team consisting of a forester, an agriculturist, a social science specialist, and an

---

[3]The Good Roots model has been incorporated into several Philippine Department of Environment and Natural Resources (DENR) projects on agriculture, forestry, and coastal marine research and development.

extension specialist. Time has shown that this is a very good mix of personnel for a project like Good Roots. In interviewing potential researchers, they found that it was important to identify individuals who not only were competent but who were self confident enough not to be threatened in a team situation. Those people should be ones who have had enough experience to recognize the limitations of a "bureaucratic mentality." Because Ilocano is the lingua franca of the region, they also decided that these researchers ideally should be native Ilocano speakers and from the general region of the area where the project was to be conducted. Selecting researchers who already had some familiarity with the research area greatly reduced the time needed to adjust to the field situation.

Even though each team member brings a particular specialty to the project and has primary responsibility in his or her arena, the actual responsibilities involve much more. While the personnel are not fully interchangeable parts of the whole, they function effectively in roles for which they were not originally trained. Each team member has trained colleagues in the fundamentals of his or her discipline in such a way that the social scientist, for example, can function with minimal help in some agricultural research. The forester can function effectively in some social science research. The agriculturist has not been fully trained as a social scientist. However, he has learned sufficient skills in social science research to carry out specific research tasks or to serve as an assistant on a particular task. The same is also true of the other researchers on the team. For example, when the forester is not propagating plants or establishing plant nurseries, he may be assisting the social scientist in conducting socioeconomic surveys or interviewing farmers on the social aspects of farming. When the social scientist is not interviewing farmer participants, she may be assisting the agriculturist in inventorying the usable plant species in the area. If the extension specialist is not busy assisting farmers in organizing themselves into work groups, she may be tabulating economic and botanical data. Drawing from a carefully structured but flexible research design, they make decisions in research and development implementation by consensus with the appropriately trained scientist providing guidance. In Good Roots, the team is the responsible unit, not individuals. Relying on a Multipurpose Research Team (MPRT) eliminates down time, redundancy, and builds *esprit de corps* leading to productivity. Personnel from the Philippine Department of Environment and Natural Resources (DENR) also are involved in monitoring the activities of the flexible research design. In the few cases where consensus cannot be reached, the director makes the decision.

The multipurpose concept along with other cost-saving measures has been applied to numerous aspects of the Good Roots project. First, the project has no office building or suite of offices. Instead, it is operated out of a modest rented house in the project area that serves as an office and also as living quarters for all project personnel. In general, based on the Good Roots experience, the benefits of the team working and living together in the same facility greatly overshadow any problems. An added benefit to this aspect of the multipurpose approach is the savings in overhead expenses. The overhead expenses for Good Roots, around 7% of the total budget, is significantly lower than many international donor projects. In some cases, the latter permit up to 25% of the budget for overhead activity.

Nursery costs also have been minimized. Good Roots nurseries are located on plots of land that were not used previously for productive farming activity. One surrounds the office/dwelling of the research team on land that is a yard area. One or two nurseries are located in each of the four research villages. In those cases the communities provide space for the nurseries as a part of their contribution to Good Roots. Importantly, the benefits from the nurseries and the Good Roots Agroforestry Association come about at little or no financial cost to the project.

A final cost-saving measure contributing to the effectiveness of Good Roots is in compensation provided to the farm family participants for their labor and time. Unlike some development projects, especially forestry projects, Good Roots participants do not receive money for working in the nurseries or for planting trees. This is antithetical to the multipurpose foundation on which the project is based. Good Roots was never intended to be nor has it become a "plant for pay" project. The Good Roots farmers are full participants and integral parts of all development activity. It is the Good Roots farm families who are improving their farming system and reclaiming their environment. They are the beneficiaries of their own labors, which is sufficient payment for them.

Conclusions

The Good Roots multipurpose model may not be suitable for all research and development projects in agroforestry. However, it is an interdisciplinary model that has proven to be successful in one region of the northern Philippines. Farmers and researchers are cooperating to bring stability to a region under environmental degradation. Their cooperation reestablishes a balance between people and nature within a reasonable time frame and at a reasonable cost. Scholars and researchers may disagree on the exact approach to be followed but many will agree that it will take an interdisciplinary-based research effort to address the environmental problems characterizing all regions of the world. The Good Roots experience suggests that, in certain situations, a multipurpose research and development model may correct the disciplinary constraints that retard the potential of interdisciplinary research and development.

References Cited

CGIAR. 1978. *Farming Systems Research at the International Research Centers.* Washington, D.C.: Consultative Group on International Agricultural Research.

De Walt, B. R. 1985. Anthropology, Sociology, and Farming Systems Research. *Human Organization* 44:106–114.

Jones, J. R., and B. J. Wallace, eds. 1986. *Social Sciences and Farming Systems Research: Methodological Perspectives on Agricultural Development.* Boulder and London: Westview Press.

Norman, D., D. H. Gilbert, and F. Winch. 1979. *Farming Systems Research for Agricultural Development.* Washington, D.C.: U.S. Agency for International Development.

Rhoades, R. E. 1985. Farming Systems Research. *Human Organization* 44:215–218.

Shaner, W. W., P. F. Philipp, and W. R. Schmehl. 1982. *Farming Systems Research and Development: Guidelines for Developing Countries.* Boulder, Colo.: Westview Press.

Von Carlowitz, P. G. 1984. Multipurpose Trees and Shrubs: Opportunities and Limitations. Working Paper No. 17. Nairobi, Kenya: International Council for Research in Agroforestry.

Wallace, B. J. 1989. Multipurpose Tree Species: A Perspective on On-Farm Research Priority and Design. In S. Sukmana, P. Amir, and D. M. Mulyadi (eds.), *Development in Procedures for Farming Systems Research, International Workshop, 1989, Bogor, Indonesia,* 146–157. Jakarta, Indonesia: Agency for Agricultural Research and Development.

Chapter 4

Why Southeast Asian Negritos are a Disappearing People: A Case Study of the Agta of Eastern Luzon, Philippines

Thomas N. Headland

A number of Negrito tribal groups are found in Southeast Asia, most of which are classified as hunter-gatherers or, more correctly, "former" hunter-gatherers. James Eder (1987) is right when he refers to them as being "on the road to tribal extinction." They are far fewer in number today than they were on the eve of European expansion. The four Negrito groups in the Andaman Islands have suffered severe depopulation in the last hundred years. The largest group there, the Onge, "have dwindled from a thousand [in 1901] to 96 today" (Updahyay 1988:88). The members of the Negrito societies in Peninsular Malaysia presently number only 2,000, far less than they numbered in the nineteenth century.

Most of the Asian Negrito populations are found in the Philippines, where there are thirty-three different populations living on several islands; two of these groups are recently extinct. (See table 4.1.) These Philippine Negritos, numbering an estimated 33,000 people today, have also greatly declined since the early Hispanic period, from around 10% of the Philippine population then, to only 0.05% of the nation's population today. One Agta Negrito ethnolinguistic population has gone extinct since the 1950s (Grimes 2000:599), and another numbering only thirty members in 1977 was down to "only twelve remaining speakers" in 1990 (Reid 1994:40);[1] and the Casiguran Agta suffered a 40% population decline between 1936 and 1984 (Headland 1989). The decline of Asia's Negritos is due to high mortality rates, not low birth rates or out-migration. These high death rates result from encroachment by outsiders, deforestation, depletion of traditional game and plant resources, increasing alcoholism, new forces introducing general poverty and new diseases, and cases of outright land-grabbing, murders, and kidnappings.

---

[1]These are the Dicamay Agta and the Aglipay Arta, in Isabela and Quirino Provinces, respectively. Both Grimes's and Reid's data come from T. Headland's field notes and Reid's fieldwork in Aglipay in 1990.

Table 4.1. Negrito languages spoken in the Philippines

(Compiled by Thomas N. Headland, April 2002)

Language Name	Population Size in 1990s	Bibliographic Source
Batak, Palawan Island	386	Eder 1987
Mamanwa, Mindanao Island	1000	Grimes 2000
Ati, northern Panay Island	30	Pennoyer 1987:4
Ati, southern Panay Island	900	Pennoyer 1987:4
Ata, Negros Island	450	Cadelina 1980:96
Ata, Mabinay, Negros Oriental	25	Grimes 2000
Atta, Pamplona, western Cagayan	1000	Grimes 2000
Atta, Faire-Rizal, western Cagayan	400	Grimes 2000
Atta, Pudtol, Kalinga-Apayao	100	Grimes 2000
Ayta, Sorsogon	40	Grimes 2000
Agta, Villa Viciosa, Abra, NW Luzon (extinct?)	0	Grimes 2000; Reid, per. com. 2001
Ayta groups of western Luzon:		
Abenlen, Tarlac	6000	K. Storck SIL files
Mag-anchi, Zambales, Tarlac, Pampang	4166	K. Storck SIL files
Mag-indi, Zambales, Pampanga	3450	K. Storck SIL files
Ambala, Zambales, Pampanga, Bataan	1654	K. Storck SIL files
Magbeken, Bataan	381	K. Storck SIL files
Agta groups of Sierra Madre, eastern Luzon		
Agta, Isarog, Camarines Sur (language nearly extinct)	1000	Grimes 2000
Agta, Mt. Iraya and Lake Buhi east, Camarines Sur (4 close dialects)	200	Grimes 2000
Agta, Mt. Iriga and Lake Buhi west, Camarines Sur	1500	Grimes 2000
Agta, Camarines Norte	200	Grimes 2000
Agta, Alabat Island, southern Quezon	50	Grimes 2000
Agta, Umirey, Quezon (3 close dialects)	3000	T. MacLeod SIL files
Agta, Casiguran, northern Aurora	609	Headland 1989
Agta, Maddela, Quirino	300	Headland field notes
Agta, Palanan and Divilacan, Isabela	856	Rai 1990:176
Agta, San Mariano-Disabungan, Isabela	377	Rai 1990:176
Agta, Dicamay, Jones, Isabela (recently extinct),	0	Headland field notes; Grimes 2000
Arta, Aglipay, Quirino (pop. was 30 in 1977)	12	Headland field notes; Reid 1994:40.
Alta, Northern, Aurora	250	Reid, per. comm.
Alta, Southern, Quezon	400	Reid, per. comm.
Agta, eastern Cagayan, Dupaninan (several close dialects)	1200	T. Nickell 1985:119
Agta, central Cagayan	800	Mayfield 1987:vii–viii; Grimes 2000
33 known no. of Negrito languages in Philippines	**32,726** =	**total estimated number of Negritos in Philippines**

Fifteen separate Agta Negrito populations live in the Sierra Madre today, each speaking its own language or dialect. (See table 4.1, and for details Headland and Griffin 1997.) They total some 11,000 people. Traditionally, they live mainly by hunting and gathering forest products, although they also do some small-scale slash-and-burn cultivation. The Agta are the original possessors of the Sierra Madre mountain range of eastern Luzon. They were its original and sole inhabitants for thousands of years before the first non-Negrito peoples (the ancestors of almost all Filipinos) began their migrations into the Philippines 5,000 years ago.

Why Negrito Societies Are Disappearing

This essay focuses on why the Agta, and all Southeast Asian Negrito societies, are disappearing today. Three main reasons are presented here: First, the natural resources on which the Negrito peoples have depended for many thousands of years have been all but destroyed in the last half-century. Second, because even when outside agencies try to help such post-foraging societies they too often impose their aid in ethnocentric ways that do more harm than good. And third, because of outright abuse—outsiders violate the human rights of the Negritos. The problems are illustrated from case studies of the Agta Negritos of eastern Luzon, and especially from the Casiguran Agta population in northern Aurora.

Reason One: Destruction of the Philippine forests

As the Philippine nation enters the twenty-first century, its people and its leaders face many overwhelming challenges. In my view as an ecological anthropologist, the most challenging problem of the Filipino people is not economic, but environmental. Its leaders must find a way to preserve their people's dwindling natural resources. The nation, in fact, sits on the very edge of a major ecological crisis. One part of that problem is the population explosion. These 7,000 islands comprised less than a million people when Europeans first arrived in the 1500s. By 1900 the population had climbed to 8 million, and today (2002) there are over 78 million people with the projection to grow another 40% by 2025 to 108 million. These are frightening figures for a nation with a land area of only 116,000 square miles (300,000 square kilometers).

The Agta rainforest has not been spared from this "Quiet Apocalypse" that is going on today throughout the Philippines. Before World War II the Casiguran lowlands of northern Aurora were 80% covered by old-growth forest. By 1990 the area covered by such full-closure forest was reduced to 9% (NAMRIA 1991:52). When my wife, Janet Headland, and I were there in 2000, we estimated that such forest area is now reduced to 3%. In the last three decades, many thousands of non-Agta Filipino lowlanders have spilled across the nation's last frontier, the mountain ridges of the Sierra Madre, into northern Aurora, so that today they outnumber the Agta 85 to 1. Today, with their traditional forest resources depleted, the Agta have modified their economic behavior; hunting has all but disappeared, and wage labor for non-Agta lowlanders has become their main way of making a living. It is this deforestation that has transformed the Agta people from foragers to landless peasants.[2] Beginning in March 1962, we have spent many years living with Agta on those eastern slopes of the Sierra Madre.[3] In the 1960s, most of the area was still dense old-growth closed-cover forest. Today, with loggers, miners, and immigrant farmers moving into the remotest areas of the Sierra Madre, the so-called "virgin" forest is all but gone.

Reason Two: Imposed community "development"

We turn to applied anthropology to illustrate a second reason for the problem. Let me begin by telling a true story, a story that I personally witnessed. Several years ago a private organization arranged a community aid project near the municipality of Casiguran, Aurora, to help the Agta Negrito people in the area. The Philippine military had recently evacuated fifteen Agta families from their homes in the forest to a temporary reservation one kilometer from the town. It was felt that this was a necessary transfer because antigovernment guerrilla activity in the mountains had made the forest area dangerous even for the Agta. Since these Agta were taken away from their usual source of livelihood and were relocated near the town, it seemed an opportune time to organize a social aid program for them.

Since the Agta children were suffering from malnutrition, the first step in the program was a decision to feed all of these children one nourishing meal a day. The program supervisors decided to have this meal served at noon each day to all of the children. This hour was chosen because the non-Agta women from the town, who volunteered to prepare the food, were free of their own home responsibilities at that time. They built a thatch-roofed shelter on the Agta reservation with a long bamboo table on which to serve the children. For the first three or four meals all of the children turned out, but after that very few children showed up for these noon mealtimes, and food went to waste. The town women who had volunteered to do the cooking, and the development agent who was supervising the program, were compassionate people. They honestly wanted to help their displaced countrymen. Nevertheless, they soon became discouraged with the Agta and their apparent lack of interest in seeing their children fed. The lunches being served were nutritious (rice, meat or fish, vegetables, and fruits). Those supervising the program finally decided that it was useless to continue because

---

[2]The negative effects of tropical deforestation on indigenous forest peoples worldwide are discussed in Sponsel, Headland, and Bailey (1996). For details on the Agta's problems, see Headland (1988), and Early and Headland (1998). For an exhaustive review of the recent political-economic-ecological changes in the Sierra Madre, see Top (1998).

[3]Between 1962 and 1986 Janet Headland and I spent eighteen years in the Philippines, with most of that time in Agta fieldwork. Since 1986, we have conducted short periods of Agta fieldwork in 1992, 1994, 1995, 1998, 2000, and 2002.

"the G-stringed pagans were too ignorant to see the value" of such a project. The program was dropped.

What went wrong with the free lunch project?

Why did this community aid project fail? This is an important question for any development planners if they are serious about helping the Agta, or any other poor community of people in a cross-cultural setting. The first problem with the free lunch project is simple. It had to do with the diet that was served. Although the food was indigenous to the area, its method of preparation followed the recipes of the town people rather than that of the Agta. The second day that the meal was served, the vegetable was boiled squash mixed with canned milk. Several Agta mothers complained that this caused their children to have diarrhea—not surprising, since most Agta lack the enzyme lactase, which means they cannot digest milk. On the third day, pork was served. Although the children ate the pork, their parents were repulsed. The Agta eat wild pig, but consider the meat of domesticated pig repugnant.

The main reason the project failed, however, was that the supervisor of the project insisted that the meals be served at noon, in spite of the parents' suggestion that it be served at breakfast or at the evening meal. Agta traditionally go off to work away from their homes for the whole day, taking their children with them. Consequently, the only way the parents could get their children to the noon meal was for them to stay home themselves for the whole day, which they could not afford to do, or to leave the children behind in the village to fend for themselves, which they were reluctant to do.

Application of community development principles

If a cross-cultural aid project is not designed to appeal to the important values held by the people of the client community, and to conform to their established patterns of daily living and social structure, it has little hope of success. The development worker must organize the program in such a way that it will "fit" the convenience and the culture of the client society, rather than the agent's own convenience (Foster 1973:164–174). For example, the timing of the free meal did not fit into the cultural patterns of the Agta because it was at noontime. The agent supervising the above program was unable to see this problem and was, not unlike the rest of us, hindered by his own ethnocentric biases. This resulted in resentment towards the Agta, which made him unable to see them as anything other than people who were unwilling to cooperate with his humanitarian aid to them.

Whenever one wishes to introduce a community aid project, there are basic principles that must be applied if the agent wishes to see his project succeed. A basic principle that was violated in this case study is what anthropologist Ward Goodenough calls "cooperation in change." Goodenough's thesis simply says that in any program of community aid the proposal must have the cooperation of the client society in order to succeed. Goodenough suggests that "the agent and community [must] work closely together in both the formulation and organization of a program [if it is to succeed]" (1963:365). The agent in the free lunch study not only failed to secure the cooperation of the Agta, but he even rejected the parents' request that the meals be served to their children at a more convenient time. Unfortunately, noon was the convenient time for the agent, and so that was the time chosen.

Implications for change agencies

If Filipino national or provincial leaders are genuinely interested in helping groups like the Agta, the first need is for their land rights to be secured. They should be given ownership of their own traditional ancestral domain. This is a tall order, a difficult task. It is for this reason that I congratulate the Philippines for passing the *Indigenous Peoples Rights Act* in October 1997. This moral decision has won esteem and respect for the Philippine government from anthropologists and human rights organizations around the world. This took great courage, as the bill went through months of debate in the Philippine Congress before it was finally passed. For those readers not from the Philippines, this is Republic Act 8371, signed into law by then-President Fidel Ramos on October 29, 1997. Popularly called "IPRA"—the *Indigenous Peoples Rights Act*—it is also referred to as the Ancestral Domain Law. This law recognizes, protects, and promotes the rights of the indigenous peoples in the Philippines. The law seeks to stop prejudices against them through the recognition of certain rights over their ancestral lands, and the right to live their lives in accordance with their indigenous traditions, religions, and customs. It is hoped that with the enactment of this law that the Philippine indigenous peoples will now be able to eventually join the mainstream of Philippine society in community development and nation building.

As President Ramos himself stated in a news release from his office dated October 29, 1997, it is "a triumph of political will." "It took courage," he stated, "to have this law passed in the midst of opposition from many influential groups whose interests would be diminished by returning ancestral rights to our indigenous communities."

This law came under serious attack in 1998 by a few influential people who claim that parts of the law are unconstitutional (Pabico 1998). This charge led to the filing of a lawsuit with the Supreme Court against the IPRA in October 1998. While the arguments of these opponents must be heard respectfully, it is my hope that the Philippine government will retain the moral courage it showed the world in 1997 to do what is right for the poorest of the poor in that nation. While a final ruling has still not been made, the Supreme Court, after two years of debate, on December 6, 2000, did finally "junk" the petition questioning the constitutionality of IPRA (Visto 2000).

Reason Three: Agta human rights violations

The third reason why Negritos are a disappearing people is the outright human rights abuses against them. This reason is more ruthless than the destruction of tropical forests or the ethnocentric misapplications of economic development programs, illustrated here with case study examples of heartless brutality against the Agta people.[4]

U.S. Army captain chain-gangs Agta for slave labor

The earliest abuse case on record was when a U.S. Army officer, Capt. Wilfrid Turnbull, stationed in Casiguran in the 1910s, forcibly moved the Agta onto a reservation and actually chain-ganged reluctant men together to get them to clear fields for cultivation (Turnbull 1930:40).

Land takeover by a mining company

Another human rights case that caused devastating upheaval to one band of Agta occurred in the Dinapigui Valley, then part of the municipality of Casiguran, when the transnational Acoje Mining Company opened a magnesium open pit mine there in 1960. The company brought in large numbers of immigrants as employees. Many of these employees remained as permanent homestead farmers after the mine was closed down in the early 1970s. The manager of the Acoje mine, who was an American, drove the Agta from their land in 1960, destroying their houses and crops with bulldozers to make room for the company's buildings. Today the forest in that valley is gone and the whole area is dotted with farms. The Agta who once lived there are gone.

Two massacres at Agta camps

One of the worst cases of Agta human rights violations occurred in the 1940s about thirty kilometers west of the town of Casiguran on the west side of the Sierra Madre. According to our Agta friends, a group of farmers led by a man named Rafael, with the nickname of Paeng, made a surprise attack on a camp of Agta. Three older Agta men, two of whom were in the camp at the time (and one of whom has a large scar from a bullet wound he received then), gave us in separate interview sessions detailed descriptions of the incident. My wife and I have confirmed that at least twenty-three Agta adults, plus several children, were massacred in this attack.[5] Another massacre at an Agta camp occurred more recently, in 1985. On the afternoon of December 12, a government

---

[4]For more details and bibliographic references of the following case studies of Agta human rights violations, see Headland and Headland (1997).

[5]We have three lists of names of alleged victims, elicited from these three informants in separate interview sessions. The total number of names comes to thirty-six, but only twenty-three of them appear in all three lists. We are less sure of the thirteen names of victims that only one man claimed to know. All three stated they could not remember the names of several children killed.

military unit of five soldiers attacked an Agta family on the Pinamakan River, in Casiguran, killing four Agta—a man, his wife, and two of their children. A third son, fourteen years old, was wounded in the leg, but escaped.[6]

Soldiers' treatment of Agta prisoners

This was not the only case of the abuse of Agta by soldiers during our tenure. In 1974, Lakaséw, an Agta teenage male, was caught allegedly stealing rice from a storeroom in a military camp in Casiguran. The next day, according to our source who witnessed the incident, the soldiers led Lakaséw out of their sleeping quarters and told him he could go. After he had walked a short distance down the road, they turned their rifles on him and shot him dead. In another incident, on October 9, 1978, soldiers ambushed a group of antigovernment NPA guerrillas who were in the forest in Isabela Province. A four-year-old Agta girl was killed in that skirmish and her Casiguran Agta mother was captured. We finally found the mother in confinement at a military headquarters in northern Luzon on February 13, 1979, where the soldiers were using her and another Casiguran Agta prisoner, a twenty-year-old mentally retarded woman, for sexual purposes. After some patient diplomatic efforts in government offices in Manila, the two women were released to my wife and me on April 2.[7]

The poisoning of an Agta camp in 1990

On March 11, 1990, an entire camp group of Agta were accidentally poisoned by a group of six Ilokano farmers who poured a bottle of commercial insecticide into the river 300 meters above the Agta camp. This tragic event occurred on the headwaters of the Immurung River in the municipal area of San Jose, in the Province of Cagayan. The farmers were using the insecticide to catch shrimp. Fifty of the fifty-six Agta in the camp fell ill that afternoon after drinking water from the river. Six of these Agta died by nightfall. Several others were taken by logging truck to the clinic in San Jose for treatment; and the more serious cases were transferred from there to the government hospital at Tuguegarao City. The

---

[6]This incident was related to my wife and me by several Agta, by the vice-mayor of Casiguran, by the Chief of Police, and by a military officer. We also were allowed to read, but were not given a copy of, two typed military reports of the incident. The military version was that the Agta man, Tamolan (a pseudonym), was wanted for murder, and was shot for attempting to flee when approached. The typed reports did not mention that a woman and children were also gunned down. Local civilians' version of the incident, as they related it to us, was that the military was after Tamolan for allegedly stealing a canvas tent. I sent a more detailed report of this incident, with names of the soldiers and victims, to Amnesty International in September 1986.

[7]The two women had to sign sworn affidavits typed up by the military before they could be released to us. We have copies of these affidavits, typed in English, which the women would not understand. The affidavits say, in part, "[I swear] that during my interrogation/detention, I was fairly treated and that I have no complaint whatsoever against [the military];...that I will not disclose anything that transpired during my interrogation/detention at HQ [name of military base] to the mass media unless cleared by military authorities."

farmers eventually paid an indemnity of 7,000 pesos (equivalent to $264 U.S. dollars) to the relatives of the six dead Agta. Two other Agta men suffered permanent damage to their larynxes, so that they speak today only with great difficulty.[8]

The Agta orphanage program in Cagayan

Change agents—whether government or private, American or Filipino—chronically stereotype Agta in negative terms in their written reports, often as a justification for imposing change upon them. In 1980, the government-appointed Commissioner to the Non-Christian Tribes for Cagayan Province established what he called an orphanage for Agta children near the provincial capital. Part of his program involved rounding up Agta children in that province (not in Casiguran) to live permanently at the orphanage. It is rare to find people in our day and age who would justify removing children from their parents. Yet this man appears to have viewed his "development program" as saving Agta children from what he views as a primitive and thus deplorable way of life. His 1981 report to his financial supporters in the United States describes the Agta as a "Newly Found Tribe" of "cannibal[s] in the upper Sierra Madre." He defines them as

> the most primitive, wild, fierce, and dangerous group...a generation from the Stone Age...having no clothes...Fond of eating raw food such as meat...[their] children unwanted and unloved...ignorant of days, weeks, months, as well as years...idolatry and adultery are supreme. (Cortez 1981)

He even quotes one Agta as saying, "The most delicious meat is the liver of human beings" (ibid.).

Land-grabbing of Agta fields

Without a doubt, the main human rights violation against the Agta today, while less violent than kidnapping and mass murder, is the frequent usurpation of Agta land. Cultivated land is a highly valued commodity in the Philippines today, and land in Casiguran is no exception. Though the majority of lowland Filipinos in the Casiguran area treat the Agta fairly and show respect for their property rights, still a number of people there, as in all frontier areas, are quick to take advantage of local tribal people. This is easy to do, because the Agta have virtually no political voice in eastern Luzon, and the majority ethnic group looks down on them.

Agta cannot succeed as farmers because, in almost all cases, when they clear a piece of land, it is taken over by lowlanders. This is the reason why they put so little time into farming today. In 1983, for example, my wife and I recorded nine

---

[8]The names of the six Agta who died were: Angela Cabaldo, Domi Padre, Gutok Padre, Pelipe Pasis, Bakas More, Junior, and an unnamed boy whose father's name is Esing. The two men with the damaged throats are Pelip Caronan and Ben Caronan.

cases of land disputes between Agta and non-Negrito farmers. In the same year we also mapped and recorded the histories of all of the thirty-two field sites that had been cleared since 1900 in a single river basin in one Agta band area. From 1900 to 1983, nineteen of the thirty-two sites on the Koso River were cleared and cultivated by lowland homesteaders using Agta labor; and thirteen of them were cleared by Agta for their own use. By 1983, lowlanders had taken over all but one of the thirteen sites, five by direct force. Three others the Agta were pressured to sell to farmers. In the other five cases, farmers just moved in and took over the land after the Agta had harvested their rice and were letting the land lie fallow. When we first resided in the upriver Koso watershed in 1962, the area was the exclusive domain of the Agta. Today it is completely taken over by outsiders and no Agta live there.

It has often been impossible for us to gain access to government documents concerning the Agta. My wife and I were fortunate, however, to be given access to the records of a government agent in charge of the Casiguran Agta for the four-year period from 1960 to 1963. We found in those documents, for just that short period in Casiguran, reports of thirty-nine cases of land conflicts between Agta and non-Agta farmers. Another case was the 1.53 square-kilometer land reservation established for the Agta in Casiguran (see Headland 1985) but taken over by outsiders, making it impossible for the Agta to establish themselves there. Jean Peterson (1978:9, 30, 70–71) also refers to the usurping of Agta fields by outsiders in Palanan, Isabela, 90 km. north of Casiguran, and the conflicts those Agta encountered when they tried to take up farming in that area. Bion Griffin (1991) reviews land usurpation and human rights violations in other Agta areas outside of Casiguran.

A number of archival reports from the early years of this century, as well, show how, when Casiguran Agta attempted serious cultivation, the more-powerful farming peoples interfered with them. Turnbull, the American army officer, who in 1912 was attempting to make the Agta into farmers, reports the following incident. "There was quite a little opposition on the part of a few Casiguran people to this work with the wild [Agta] people—some fearing a lack of labor, others a loss of trade as a consequence" (Turnbull 1930:32).

Turnbull was correct, but these were not the only reasons the townspeople were against his project. They were also against his helping the Agta acquire arable land of their own. Ten years after Turnbull's project began, the Casiguran Municipal Council wrote a formal resolution, titled Resolution No. 71 and dated July 14, 1923. This resolution objected to the giving of land to the Agta because, the Resolution says, it gave "them greater area of land than the Christian [i.e., non-Agta] people residing at Casiguran." The final paragraph of this document petitions the Provincial Board, the Provincial Governor, and the President of the Philippine Senate to "suspend the advance" of Agta farmland at the reservation (Casiguran Municipal Council 1923).

This problem of land grabbing has not lessened as we enter the third millennium. Rather it has become more acute as Filipinos migrate into the Sierra Madre today by the thousands. A most vivid recent example was when a single incident on New Year's Day 1994 reduced the Casiguran Agta population by another 1%. This was when a group of lowlander men ambushed an Agta family of five at Dibet, Casiguran. The Agta mother and father (Marning Bunaw and Bagéy Tapilyong) were stabbed to death and Nimpa, the youngest of their three children, was wounded in the abdomen. The three orphaned children (ages 3, 7, and 9) were taken to town where they have been permanently "adopted" into non-Agta households. The police report and the Aurora provincial newspaper (*Dawn* 1994) state that the two murdered Agta "sustained multiple wounds all over their bodies," and that the Agta were killed because they would not give up their claim to their land. The newspaper published the name of one of the alleged killers, a local Bikolano homesteader, but as of April 1994 he had not been arrested.

The two government-designated Agta land reservations

Two political decisions in favor of the Casiguran Agta were achieved in the 1930s. In 1934 the 1.53 square-kilometer Calabgan reservation established by Turnbull twenty years earlier and cleared and cultivated by Agta at that time (Worcester 1913; Lukban 1914; Whitney 1914; Government Printing Office 1916; Sanvictores 1923) was formally declared "for the exclusive use of the [Agta] non-Christians" by Governor General Proclamation No. 723. This document (Governor General 1935:955–957) was signed and sealed by Governor General Frank Murphy on August 21, 1934. It defines in detail the exact borders of the reservation.

In 1939, another large area of land in Casiguran was set aside for the Agta, at Kasapsapan Bay (twenty kilometers northwest of the Calabgan reservation). This area, comprising 62.69 hectares, was formally reserved for the exclusive use of the non-Christian Agta by Presidential Proclamation No. 467, signed by Philippine President Manuel L. Quezon on October 9, 1939 (Quezon 1939:748–749).

Sadly, both of these areas deeded to the Agta were by the 1970s taken over by non-Agta outsiders. The complex details of these two land conflicts are described in detail elsewhere (Headland and Headland 1997:86–88). The Agta lost out every time disputes came up over the two land areas.

Conclusion

This chapter has attempted to explain three main reasons why Southeast Asian Negritos are a disappearing people. Three main reasons have been outlined. These Negrito cultures, and specifically the Agta Negritos of eastern Luzon, are disappearing because their forests are being destroyed; because outsiders violate their human rights and land rights; and because in the few cases where well-meaning outsiders want to aid them, they impose on the Negritos so-called development that is ethnocentric and that is made to fit the convenience of the national society rather than the culture of the Negritos. We are not arguing here for trying to preserve Negritos in some kind of a static, pre-contact cultural way of life; nor are we trying to say that cultural change is bad. Indeed, as humanity today—including traditional indigenous peoples everywhere—enters the third millennium, it would be the height of naiveté to think that tribal peoples now will want to go back to living as their grandparents did. Most do not. In 1992 when some wealthy American environmentalists criticized the Brazilian Kayapó Indians for selling the hardwood trees on their reservation to loggers, the Kayapó responded by saying that they spend most of their money on necessities such as food, medicines, and schools. They asked the environmentalists why, if they wish to live like other Brazilians, they are looked on as absurd, immoral, and wrong (Epstein 1993). Good question.

We are only saying that indigenous peoples should be allowed the freedom to change as they wish, at the speed they wish, without violation of their human rights. There is nothing bad about outside change agents helping traditional indigenous peoples, but as Goodenough tried to tell us forty years ago, there must be "cooperation in change," not imposed change, if it is to help the poorest of the poor in the third millennium.

References Cited

Cadelina, Rowe V. 1980. Adaptive Strategies to Deforestation: The Case of the Ata of Negros Island, Philippines. *Silliman Journal* 27:93–112.

Casiguran Municipal Council. 1923. Extract from the Minutes of the Regular Session Held by the Municipal Council of Casiguran on the 14th Day of July 1923. [Typescript, 2 pages, signed by Pedro C. Valencia, Municipal Secretary. Archived in the Manuel L. Quezon Papers, Series VII, Box 136, folder for 1922–1923; in the Rare Books and Manuscripts Section, Filipiniana Division, National Library, Manila.]

Cortez, C. R. 1981. The Newly Found Tribe. [Published in 1981 in an undated 4-page published report of the *Philippine Native Crusade* (Rt. 2, Box 279, Bradenton, Florida 33505, and Box 121, Tuguegarao, Cagayan, Philippines).]

Dawn. 1994. "Masaker!" [English: 'Massacre']. *The Dawn: Balita sa Aurora* [official newspaper of Aurora Province] 3(35):17–23 (January).

Early, John D., and Thomas N. Headland. 1998. *Population Dynamics of a Philippine Rain Forest People: The San Ildefonso Agta.* Gainesville: University Press of Florida.

Eder, James F. 1987. *On the Road to Tribal Extinction.* Berkeley: University of California Press.

Epstein, Jack. 1993. Brazil Indians Defend Sale of Gold, Trees. *The Dallas Morning News,* November 6, 1993, p. 20A.

Foster, George M. 1973. *Traditional Societies and Technological Change.* 2nd edition. New York: Harper and Row.

Goodenough, Ward H. 1963. *Cooperation in Change.* New York: Russel Sage Foundation.

Government Printing Office. 1916. *Report of the Philippine Commission.* Washington, D.C.: Government Printing Office.

Governor General. 1935. *Executive Orders and Proclamations: Issued by the Governor-General During the Year 1934.* Manila: Bureau of Printing.

Griffin, P. Bion. 1991. Philippine Agta Forager-Serfs: Commodities and Exploitation. *Senri Ethnological Studies* 30:199–222.

Grimes, Barbara F. 2000. *Ethnologue: Volume 1: Languages of the World.* 14th edition. Dallas: SIL International.

Headland, Thomas N. 1985. Imposed Values and Aid Rejection among Casiguran Agta. In P. Bion Griffin and Agnes Estioko-Griffin (eds.), *The Agta of Northeastern Luzon: Recent Studies,* 102–118. Cebu City, Philippines: University of San Carlos.

Headland, Thomas N. 1988. Ecosystemic Change in a Philippine Tropical Rain Forest and its Effect on a Negrito Foraging Society. *Tropical Ecology* 29 (2):121–135.

Headland, Thomas N. 1989. Population Decline in a Philippine Negrito Hunter-Gatherer Society. *American Journal of Human Biology* 1:59–72.

Headland, Thomas N., and P. Bion Griffin. 1997. A Bibliography of the Agta Negritos of Eastern Luzon, Philippines. *SIL Electronic Working Papers* 1997–004. Dallas: Summer Institute of Linguistics.
http://www.sil.org/silewp/1997/004/silewp1997–004.html (June 20, 2002).

Headland, Thomas N., and Janet D. Headland. 1997. Limitation of Human Rights, Land Exclusion, and Tribal Extinction: The Agta Negritos of the Philippines. *Human Organization* 56:79–90.

Lukban, Vicente. 1914. Report del Gobernador de Tayabas Hon. Vicente Luckban [sic] al Secretario del Interior Hon. Winfred T. Denison Sombre [sic] la Cuestión de las Tribus Infieles en Dicha Provincia. In *Ethnography of the Negrito-Aeta Peoples,* Vol. 2, Paper No. 50, H. Otley Beyer (compiler), 1918. [Typescript, 13 pages. Manila; a microfilm collection of original sources.] Harvard University Microfilm Dept. Harvard order no. 65-60-38.

Mayfield, Roy. 1987. *Central Cagayan Agta Texts.* Studies in Philippine Linguistics (Supplementary Series: Philippine Texts No. 2). Manila: Linguistic Society of the Philippines and Summer Institute of Linguistics.

NAMRIA. 1991. *Report on Forest Cover Survey and Mapping of Aurora Province.* Manila: National Mapping and Resource Information Authority.

Nickell, Thomas L. 1985. A Partial Stratification Analysis of Eastern Cagayan Agta Language. In P. Bion Griffin and Agnes A. Estioko-Griffin (eds.), *The Agta of Northeastern Luzon: Recent Studies,* 119–146. Cebu City, Philippines: University of San Carlos Publications.

Pabico, Alecks P. 1998. *Landmark Law on Indigenous Peoples Hits a Dead End.* Philippine Center for Investigative Journalism. http://www.pcij.org/stories/1998/ipra.html (June 21, 2002).

Pennoyer, F. Douglas. 1987. Inati: The Hidden Negrito Language of Panay, Philippines. *Philippine Journal of Linguistics* 17(2) and 18(1):1–36.

Peterson, Jean T. 1978. *The Ecology of Social Boundaries: Agta Foragers of the Philippines.* Urbana: University of Illinois Press.

Quezon, Manuel L. 1939. *Executive Orders and Proclamations: Issued by the Governor-General During the Year 1939.* Manila: Bureau of Printing. Reprinted in *Official Gazette* 37(131):2719 (November 2, 1939).

Rai, Navin K. 1990. *Living in a Lean-to: Philippine Negrito Foragers in Transition.* Ann Arbor: University of Michigan Museum of Anthropology.

Reid, Lawrence A. 1994. Possible Non-Austronesian Lexical Elements in Philippine Negrito Languages. *Oceanic Linguistics* 33:37–72.

Sanvictores, Jose G. 1923. [One-page letter typed in English, addressed to the Secretary of the Interior, and signed by Sanvictores, Director of the Bureau of Non-Christian Tribes, in Manila, dated July 21, 1923. Original letter archived in the Manuel L. Quezon Papers, in the Rare Books and Manuscripts Room, Filipiniana Division, National Library (Manila), Box 163.]

Sponsel, Leslie E., Thomas N. Headland, and Robert C. Bailey (eds). 1996. *Tropical Deforestation: The Human Dimension.* New York: Columbia University Press.

Top, Gerhard van den. 1998. *The Social Dynamics of Deforestation in the Sierra Madre, Philippines.* Leiden: Centre of Environmental Science, Leiden University.

Turnbull, Wilfrid. 1930. Bringing a Wild Tribe under Government Control. *Philippine Magazine* 26(12):782–783, 794, 796, 798; 27(1):31–32, 36, 38, 40, 42; 27(2):90–91, 116–118, 120.

Updahyay, V.S. 1988. Is Retrieval from the Precipice Possible? A Case Study of Onge of Little Andamans (India). In *Abstracts: 12th International Congress of Anthropological and Ethnological Sciences,* Vol. 12, 87–88. Zagreb: Croatian Anthropological Society, University of Zagreb.

Visto, Cecille S. 2000. Case vs Indigenous People's Right to Claim Land Junked by High Court. *Businessworld* 8–9 (December). http://www.geocities.com/ferdibee/ipralaw.htm (June 20, 2002).

Whitney, Capt. F[rancis]. A. 1914. [Letter to the Provincial Governor of Nueva Vizcaya, dated March 15, 1914. Archived in the Dean C. Worcester Papers (Box 1, folder labeled "Correspondence, July-Sept 1914"). Michigan Historical Collections, University of Michigan, Bentley Historical Library, Ann Arbor, Michigan.]

Worcester, Dean C. 1913. *Annual Report of the Secretary of the Interior: For the Fiscal Year Ended June 30, 1913.* Manila: Bureau of Printing.

Chapter 5

Change and Resilience among the Agta of Isabela and Cagayan Provinces, the Philippines

P. Bion Griffin

The present chapter overviews the probable trajectory of changes experienced by the Agta, a formerly mobile group of foragers, variously called Negritos, Dumagats, Aeta, Pugot, and other names. The people call themselves Agta. The main thesis of the chapter is that Agta have been changing to meet internally- and externally-generated demands for thousands of years, and that they continue, as Agta, to adapt. Further, I suggest that their ongoing behaviors involve use of the plant cover that once existed as uncut old-growth tropical rainforest. Global efforts to preserve remaining forests may provide the Agta new directions in resource manipulation.

The vast forests of the Sierra Madre that the Agta exploited for millennia are indeed gone, and their passing is properly lamented. The Agta people of eastern Luzon are, thankfully, not gone. Their culture and way of life are sorely stressed, and living off the forest remnants is increasingly problematic. As with all cultures and peoples, change is ongoing. The Agta consider some of the change as bad, but much they see as good. A forest-loving folk, Agta acknowledge that the game, riverine fish, plant foods, and the general providence of the now diminished forest have drastically decreased to the extent that a foraging or hunting-gathering way of life cannot be sustained. But, we must place the Agta of eastern Luzon into their historical contexts if we are to suggest what they will do in the future.

What Agta Did in the Past (20,000 B.P. to 1500s)

Agta culture and the behavior of its society's members have been changing since the earliest observations recorded by Spanish colonials. Of course, all cultures change over time. If anthropologists have learned anything, it is this truism. Not all change, however, is beneficial. Change often occurs in such a fashion—even when induced from within its society—that maladaption occurs and quality of life declines. More often an external and likely dominant people impose new conditions that must be met and adjusted to. We are interested in how the people who now identify themselves as Agta will maintain themselves in the twenty-first century. In short, now that their forest-based way of life has been marginalized, are they slated to merge with an impoverished peasantry, recognizable only through subtleties of variation in hair and skin color, or will an Agta culture endure? Will the rapacious external forces that have ruined the Philippine forests continue their destructive course, or will the Agta co-opt new forces for their own benefit and power?

Early in the sixteenth century, Agta culture had already endured for unknown millennia and had undergone massive and perhaps traumatic changes. Anthropological linguists, archaeologists, and scholars of the Philippine Aeta groups argue that, at some point perhaps in the late Pleistocene, the ancestors of today's Agta and of all Aeta[1] migrated into the archipelago via Palawan, moving on foot through Sundaland until reaching the then Mindoro-Luzon water barrier. No evidence exists that assigns these migrants other than forager status; plant manipulation seemingly did not reach the level of cultivation and domestication of food resources. Given a highly mobile life style, an effective hunting and riverine fishing technology, coupled with exploitation of plant resources, the ancestral Agta changed only slowly until the arrival of technologically more varied and dominant Proto-Austronesian speakers who sailed to Luzon's coasts about 5,000 years ago. One might speculate that this arrival was as traumatic and carried as far-reaching consequences as the arrival of global capitalism in the late twentieth century. The new arrivals are thought to have been swidden root-crop and rice farmers, potters, and animal husbanders with chickens and pigs. Over centuries the original Agta language likely disappeared, and an ancient form of the several dialects of the proto-Austronesian language developed.[2] In this process a fundamental component of Agta culture may have formed, the subordinate, dependent social and economic relationship with the swidden farmers.[3] The basis of the relationship was the Agta's acquisition of cultivated plant foods such as rice in exchange for wild meats and labor in non-Agta fields. What an incredible change of lifeways this must have been! From absolute freedom to dependency and subservience! Any view of Agta culture and its preservation today must dwell on this foundation. Mobility was surely constrained those thousands of years ago; movement and residence far from

---

[1]The term *Aeta* glosses all of the short, dark-skinned formerly foraging peoples of the Philippines. Agta, by extension, are one group of *Aeta*; and the Agta themselves today are comprised of at least ten ethnolinguistic subgroups. The term *Negrito* is commonly used for *Aeta*, although I prefer to avoid the term, considering it too loaded with colonial and potentially racist content. In any case, one may assume, without a great body of data to provide support, that these people's ancestors occupied the archipelago prior to the arrival of Proto-Austronesian speakers.

[2]Most linguists and historians on the Philippines are in agreement with the model that the ancestors of today's Agta migrated into the Philippines at least 20,000 years ago. Much later, when they began interethnic relationships with early Austronesian immigrants before the time of Christ, they lost their original languages and adopted various dialects of the Austronesians. For details, see Reid (1987, 1994).

[3]While this Agta/farmer interdependent view is generally accepted among Filipinists, I am less than certain. The language adoption seems reasonable. Other explanations for the intergroup social relations seen since A.D. 1900 may be hypothesized. Space does not permit elaboration here.

non-Agta swiddener trade partners may have been impossible. The range of environments necessarily traversed was diminished, since the commitment to cultivated foodstuffs could no longer be neglected. Territories or hunting ranges changed. Dialect boundaries appeared in new forms. Gene pools changed. People adapted. Culture changed.

Activities of the Agta in the Historical Period (1600–1999)

Then the Spaniards arrived. With them came many changes. New crops from America appeared among Filipino farmers. These included maize, cassava, sweet potato, and tobacco. Swidden farmers grew in numbers along the Sierra Madre's major rivers and their arable lands. Agta culture during the Hispanic period (1565 to 1898) seems a contradiction difficult to reconcile with that known in recent years. The Spanish records suggest that Agta lived as wild, fierce, independent competitors of lowland and upland swiddeners and the new occasional hamlet dwellers (Headland 1986). In addition, some Agta seem to have maintained their own small swiddens in distant locales. But, if our model of dependence and subordinance is to hold, they cannot be seen as successfully living their own independent lives on far beaches and up remoter rivers. Or perhaps only some of the Agta fit the symbiotic interdependent mode, and, if so, why? Again, looking at Agta adaptations, we recognize continued variation over space and time. Certainly the social environment in which Agta interacted with their neighbors was becoming more complex and differentiated. Non-Agta swiddeners were becoming fixed-field farmers. Insurgents, or rebels, against the Spanish colonial masters were appearing in refuges in the Sierra Madre Mountains, and non-Agta population levels were slowly inching upward.

The first four decades of the twentieth century certainly added new strains to the lives of Agta. The American conquest of the Philippines radically changed the approach to colonial management of the islands; eastern Luzon, although relatively sheltered, was no exception (Headland 1975; Turnbull 1930; Worcester 1912). Americans brought a new approach to Christianity and a new view of the native populations. Protestant missionaries and schoolteachers reached places and peoples the Spanish never dreamed of controlling. The tribal people were symbolically and politically separated from Roman Catholic lowland Filipinos and were viewed as not unlike the Native American Indians. Both exoticized and marked for control, tribals experienced a wide range of new pressures that forced change. Agta in more accessible locations were at times moved into reservations, provided schools, and ordered to become farmers. Many Agta resisted this and opted to do otherwise. Their social and economic bonds with lowland farmers may have increased in intensity, with dependence heightened. Certainly their awareness of the larger world increased, and their vision of desirable options became clear.

World War II brought further stress, indeed crisis, to the Agta. Briefly put, Agta found themselves participants in the war, especially near the end with the retreat of Japanese soldiers into the Sierra Madre. Although they did not suffer the death and deprivation that farmers endured, they were active in killing, further establishing their fierce reputations.

The last half of the century was one of incredibly rapid change and saw the progressive loss of the forest cover. Two phenomena are linked: the post-war population explosion and the commercialization of timber extraction. Simply put, logging business devastated the valuable timber that is the heart of the forest, and poor farmers, ignorant and uncaring of proper swiddening systems, rode the logging trucks into the forest, cutting and burning tree cover of little interest to the loggers (P. B. Griffin 1985, 1991). This process fed the world's insatiable demand for wood and the farmers' need for subsistence, but it also ruined the economic basis of the Agta economy and social organization that had developed over centuries. In addition, the decades long, and presently ongoing, New People's Army insurgency against the government often affected Agta's ability to live secure and predictable life styles.

I argue, however, that no matter how much Westerners may lament the loss of the Agta adaptation, we still see the core principles working to maintain the culture. Agta adapted to loggers, guerrillas, soldiers, missionaries, anthropologists, and others who migrated into the Sierra Madre by taking advantage of them, gaining resources from them, and putting up with their—at times—unreasonable demands. As must have been the case upon the arrival of Austronesian-speaking farmers some five thousand years ago, Agta said then as they say now, "Well, life is difficult, but let's get something from this." During the 1970s and 1980s, Agta became military guides, logging scouts, provisioners for all sorts of interlopers, more or less successful farmers, fishermen, orchid collectors, and anthropological/missionary assistants, as well as drunks, beggars, prostitutes, and general failures. No doubt exists that they are an exploited and marginalized, indeed despised, people, who many Filipinos consider non-humans and entirely worth exterminating in the fashion that White Americans sought to exterminate Native Americans and that White Australians sought to kill off Aborigines. Still, the Agta adapt and readapt to new changes, including loss of the forest that was the central part of their existence for millennia.

What Will the Agta Do Next? (The Third Millennium)

An ability to adapt to new conditions in the past is no guarantee that the Agta will be successful in the future. Agta language loss is a potential problem, but they have lost and gained language once before (when they began interethnic relations with the early Austronesian settlers). And, as they attached themselves to technologically more complex Austronesian immigrants millennia ago, they have been doing the same with great agility in recent years. Agta ably worked as guides, forest survey assistants, and logging crew out of Maconacon, Isabela Province, until politics, economics and armed strife destroyed the timber company after President Marcos's fall in 1986. In Palanan, Isabela, they have adopted, with the help of the organization "Christian Missions to the Unreached," an activist Christianity that assists Agta communities in asserting legal native rights to land, forest, and institutional resources (M. Griffin 1996). As the Western world's eco-preservation movement is felt, especially around Palanan, Agta strive to be decision-makers in charting their own future. They seek to gain proper access to titled land, and in some places they have succeeded, at least for the moment. They likewise know how to assert their rights to better wages when they see they have the support of external backup authority from government, missionary, or anthropological agents. Anthropological data are privileged in Philippine law in establishing land and other rights. Agta may reasonably expect to gain access to the data and their rights through manipulations of "friendly forces," especially missionaries and anthropologists.

Still, the future is bleak, as it is for many millions of people in formerly tribal or ethnic cultural communities. The Philippine's population growth is out of control. Natural resources have been stretched and broken. Marine and riverine foods have been depleted through the vilest and most destructive means of gaining short-term returns. After a respite during the Ramos administration, armed conflict is again on the rise in many sections of the country and has reappeared in alarming proportions in Agtaland. With the demise of communism and socialism, world capitalism has run amok, leaving the Third World and especially its more vulnerable populations terribly at risk.

The worst situation is perhaps the changing *social* environment of Agta. For millennia the Agta have provided services and goods that others needed, and that Agta were willing to exchange for foodstuffs and tools. The Agta must find, within the context of their foraging-oriented behavior, the resources that others have, and what may be provided to non-Agta in order to obtain them. In the early twenty-first century we all live in a service-based economy, an information economy, and a class-based economy. As surely as the local population of Hawai'i, for example, rests its income on servicing tourists and military personnel, so many of the Agta may find the means to satisfactorily and satisfyingly service a new elite. Forget not that they, through adopting strategies of subordination and service, have "worked for" socially more powerful neighbors for ages. This service has escalated since World War II, as noted above, and has the basis for readaptation into the future. Most Agta are reportedly dubious about ecotourism and ecotourists, with good reason. For all their faults, their former traditional trade partners knew them well and extended a modicum of respect. If Agta can find new respectful and generous partners, they will be off and running, working to restore what forest is possible. The trouble is, little respect is left to go around in the Philippines today.

References Cited

Griffin, Marcus B. 1996. The Cultural Identity of Foragers and the Agta of Palanan, Isabela, the Philippines. *Anthropos* 91:111–123.

Griffin, P. Bion. 1985. Population Movements and Socio-economic Change in the Sierra Madre. In P. Bion Griffin and Agnes Estioko-Griffin (eds.), *The Agta of Northeastern Luzon: Recent Studies,* 85–101. Cebu City, Philippines: University of San Carlos Press.

Griffin, P. Bion. 1991. Philippine Agta Forager-Serfs: Commodities and Exploitation. *Senri Ethnological Papers* 30:199–222.

Headland, Thomas N. 1975 The Casiguran Dumagat Today and in 1936. *Philippine Quarterly of Culture and Society* 3:245–257.

Headland. Thomas N. 1986. Why Foragers Do Not Become Farmers: A Historical Study of a Changing Ecosystem and Its Effects on a Negrito Hunter-Gatherer Group in the Philippines. Ph.D. dissertation. University of Hawai'i, Manoa.

Reid, Lawrence A. 1987. The Early Switch Hypothesis: Linguistic Evidence for Contact between Negritos and Austronesians. *Man and Culture in Oceania* 3:41–59 (Special Issue).

Reid, Lawrence A. 1994. Possible Non-Austronesian Lexical Elements in Philippine Negrito Languages. *Oceanic Linguistics* 33:37–72.

Turnbull, Wilfred. 1930. Bringing a Wild Tribe under Government Control. *Philippine Magazine* 26(12):782–798; 27(1):31–120; 27(2):90–120.

Worcester, Dean. 1912. Headhunters of Northern Luzon. *National Geographic Magazine* 23:833–930.

Chapter 6

How Many Trees Does a Forest Make?

S. H. Sohmer

Introduction

The question implicit in the title is subject to long debate. To me, it is a simple biological/ecological question. Therefore, it is not the number or kinds of trees that define a forest, but the complex and infinitesimally diverse relationships among all of the biota of that ecosystem that make it so. Coming from this perspective, it has always appeared to me that a great deal of mythology is involved with recognizing the reality of what a forest is, and that this impacts the assessment of forest loss. For example, if one's definition of a forest includes tree plantations, which are basically monocultures, then one cannot recognize the true extent of global forest loss. Mattoon (1998:20) makes a very specific point of this in *World Watch* magazine when she states that "billions of trees are being planted to meet the soaring appetite for paper, but pulp plantations are hardly forests." She also says that the key difference between natural forests and plantations is diversity: "Natural forests are some of the most diverse ecosystems on earth, but plantations—especially industrial plantations—are generally monocultures" (ibid.). This problem of interpretation is especially evident in nonbiological but sister-fields like anthropology. Non-biologists, and even biologists who have no organismal and/or ecological training literally "cannot see the forest for the trees."

In this chapter I use my knowledge of the Philippines as the example with which to make the point that natural forests are unique. They are also wonderful examples of biological interactions that are so complex that it has still not been possible, despite decades of research now aided by the power computers provide, to understand the total nature of those relationships. I also state that most of the entities that individuals call forests are in reality only greatly simplified systems that have little resemblance to the original vegetation that once covered a great deal of the land in the temperate and tropical regions of the world. It is like comparing a cornfield to a natural prairie!

Philippine Mahogany

By 1985 I had been pursuing systematic botanical studies of certain groups of flowering plants as an active botanist for nearly two decades. I had spent about five years doing fieldwork in the Philippines, and had generally taken a passionate interest in the particular groups with which I was working to the exclusion of broader issues. I was then studying a genus in the Rubiaceae, commonly known as the coffee family. This genus, called *Psychotria,* at one time was one of the most widely distributed groups of shrubs and/or small trees in the world's tropical forests; it had hundreds of species representing it in the Pacific and Southeast Asian regions alone. After completing a monograph on many of those found in Papua New Guinea, I began to work on the Philippine representatives.

In the course of this work in the early 1980s, I had already made several long collecting trips to the Philippines where, with the aid of my colleagues at the National Museum in Manila, I had come to know the situation on the ground fairly well. The enormous amount of deforestation that had already occurred and that was continuing to occur at ever-increasing rates shocked me. I already had personally observed that little or no lowland forests remained intact on most of the main islands with the then exceptions of Mindanao and Palawan.

In 1985, I attended the Pacific Science Association's Inter-Congress in Manila. One of the speakers presented an overview of the distribution of Dipterocarp species in the Philippines. The Dipterocarp family contained hundreds of species throughout Southeast Asia, and there were over fifty in the Philippines, often generically referred to in the lumber trade as Philippine mahogany. These species were the dominant members of the lowland rainforests of this part of the world. When fully mature and perhaps hundreds of years old, these huge, wonderful trees were often so wide that several men could not join arms around their trunks. The speaker showed slide after slide of maps detailing the distribution of most of those species in the Philippines. As I looked at the slides, I became increasingly perplexed since I recognized numerous places where I had been and had not been able to find any trace of original forest cover. Could I have been that wrong in what I thought I saw?

After the talk was over, I approached the speaker, introduced myself, and asked about this apparent discrepancy, assuming that this was related to my own faulty powers of observation. How was it, I asked, that most of the areas he had spoken about with such conviction concerning the present distribution of those species were to my knowledge presently deforested? Upon further questioning, it became more than apparent, to my surprise and consternation, that this individual had been using nearly verbatim a publication by a famous American botanist, E. D. Merrill, the *Enumeration of Philippine Flowering Plants* (1922–1926). Merrill's work had taken place in the first two decades of the twentieth century and this work, published after he left, was his swan song to the Philippines. The speaker giving this paper had apparently not added any new information that would have brought that half-century old work up to date. From a

Philippines that might have had 10–15 million people at the time Merrill published his work, there were then well over 60 million people. From a time when there might have been 30 to 35% of original old-growth forest left, there were then, based on my own estimate, no more than 10%.

The Origins of the Philippine Plant Inventory

With this sort of problem and other examples like it in mind, a Philippine colleague, Dr. Domingo Madulid, and I developed plans for a new flora project designed to provide up-to-date information about the flora of the Philippines. The U.S. National Science Foundation funded part of the project. For reasons that are beyond the scope or purpose of this paper, that part, although it added vital new information, never reached the level of productivity that had been predicted. However, this project provided a very vivid glimpse of the deteriorating forest situation of the Philippines, and at least created a better awareness of the problem.

I had succeeded in securing some grant money from the MacArthur Foundation to help the Philippine National Herbarium upgrade its facility. In addition, funds received from the National Science Foundation for this project, in a unique partnership with the U.S. Agency for International Development, supported what we called the Philippine Plant Inventory. This project was specifically designed to strategically cover the country's last remaining forests and document the species found therein through actual collections in duplicate that would be distributed to a number of herbaria throughout the world, with the first set remaining in the Philippines.

It was through this project that we began to see, on the ground, the vast amount of deforestation that had already occurred and the growing discrepancy between official estimates of remaining forest cover and reality. Although we had estimated that old-growth forests occupied about 10% of the total land area of the Philippines when we began this project in 1990, the actual totals were probably far less. When this project came to a halt in 1995–1996, I would estimate that there was probably less than 3% of old-growth forest remaining. Koopowitz et al. (1998) used a stochastic model based on the unpublished revision of the genus *Psychotria* in the Philippines by Sohmer. They predicted that between 24 and 56% of the indigenous Philippine flora might already be extinct, and that, at the then current rates of deforestation, most of the remaining Philippine forests will probably be extirpated by the year 2029. This is the crux of this chapter: If one does not view old-growth (natural) forests as the true forests of an area, representing an ark of biodiversity, but rather views secondary growth forests and tree plantations as "forests" in the biological/ecological sense, then estimates of remaining forest such as mine are always going to be significantly lower.

A Personal Nirvana

An example of how the pieces of an ecosystem are interdependent is vividly demonstrated by a personal experience during my research endeavors with the genus *Psychotria* in the Philippines. As stated in Sohmer (unpublished), I have recognized 113 species in this genus for the Philippines. Nearly all of these are, or were, restricted to forests of some sort. About 40% of them have not been collected since 1930, at least as evidenced by the availability of herbarium specimens. This situation is one example of the fact that species narrowly restricted to certain habitats are most in danger of extinction. However, there are widespread species of this genus in the Philippines.

Most of the few that are widespread have tolerance for disturbance and can grow outside the protection of a closed-canopy forest. However, one that I could never find in my own fieldwork, despite the fact that, based on specimens extant in the herbaria of the world, it seemed to be one of the most common species in the Philippines, was *Psychotria membranifolia* Bartl. ex DC. I had seen and studied hundreds of herbarium specimens and they were from all over the islands. Yet, I never saw it in the field—not until I went to the island of Sibuyan in the Visayas, that middle section of islands between Luzon to the north and Mindanao to the south. One of the days in the field I happened into a pristine low montane forest and there was this species as one of the most dominant species of the understory of that forest, with hundreds and hundreds of individuals!

This forest was apparently the first undisturbed old-growth forest I had been in during my work in the Philippines. It was remarkable. Then I realized that, for reasons not fully understood, this otherwise common species was the first to go when its forests are disturbed, even when such disturbance is not readily apparent to the untrained eye. How many species we have lost, not just of plants but of insects and other forms of life from this once beautifully rich set of islands will never be known. For some of the species there will only be museum evidence that they once existed.

A Brief History of Deforestation in the Philippines

In the post-Pleistocene prehistoric era as much as 93% to 96% of the land area probably contained some sort of forest. They would have been moist forests for the most part, with lowland rainforest and montane rainforest predominating. Of course, the complexity and diversity of forest types would have been very great. It is beyond the scope of this chapter to summarize the original vegetation types of the Philippines as known at the beginning of the twentieth century. It was at that time that the modern era of botanical research began in that country and there was also the explosive growth of the human population.

By the 1930s, based largely on the work of Merrill (1922–1926), it is esti-mated that about 30% of the original forests of the Philippine Archipelago was left. In 1988 as a result of the Philippine-German Forest Resource Inventory, it is estimated that there was 7% of old-growth forest left. These figures are graphically illustrated in figure 6.1 at the end of this chapter. A view of the extent of old-growth forests in Tan and Rojo (1988) presents a rather optimistic picture of fairly unbroken blocks of forest left mostly in the mountains (see figure 6.3). The actual picture was much less rosy. I used the results of the thorough ground-aerial truthing of the remaining old-growth forests in the Philippines undertaken by the Philippine Department of Environment and Natural Resources (DENR), Forest Management Bureau cited above. I then produced a map (figure 6.4) showing that the remaining forests at that time were actually bits and pieces rather than solid blocks. Today, the situation is much worse, and even those bits and pieces are mostly gone. I would guess, as already mentioned, that there is probably less than 3% of old-growth forest left now at the beginning of the twenty-first century, and the ways of life of those indigenous peoples who were dependent on those forests have been altered forever.

Cruz summarizes succinctly what has happened in the most recent decades. I will quote directly from her abstract.

Because employment opportunities are declining in urban centers of many developing countries, the expectation of pulling migrants into cities has given way to a pattern of rural-to-rural movements into unoccupied forest lands. While most of deforestation can be attributed to commercial logging, the activity by itself does not always lead to a permanent change in land use. It is the occupation of logged-over lands, and its use for agriculture by increasing numbers of rural migrants that, together with logging, has created in many developing countries a pattern of significant forest and biodiversity loss. (2000:1)

One of Cruz's conclusions is that changes must occur in the recognition of "use-rights" of indigenous peoples or there will be failure to establish a more cogent conservation policy.

I am also pleased to see that another of Cruz's conclusions is the absolute need for the delivery of family planning into the mix of community actions. This aspect is the root cause of ecological problems, and it is often sidestepped in official presentations, papers, and articles. I would go much further and bluntly state that, if population control is not strongly encouraged by policy makers, the ecological meltdown of the Philippines will continue unabated. No amount of planning, policy or programs, or infusion of money will ever have an effect on saving what is left of that country's patrimony. As one example see figure 6.2, which, based on Heaney and Relegado (1998), shows in graphic terms what happened on the island of Negros. That island's human population went from an historical and stable figure of about 100,000, where it was at the beginning of the American colonial period, to more than 3 million today. The graph also shows that the forests of the island declined in direct proportion to the growth of the human population and the conversion of much of the land to plantation agriculture.

What is even more poignant are snapshots in time showing the elimination of old-growth forests on Mindanao (see figures 6.5 and 6.6). The maps upon which these figures are based were done at the Manila Observatory under the direction of Father Peter Walpole who graciously made them available to me.

Conclusions

In my opinion there is little or no hope for Philippine forests, unless the age of miracles is still upon us. Even to save some of the remnants will be very difficult due to a combination of cultural, ethical, and policy mores that are in place. Between the apparent corruption of some public servants, the poverty and religiously induced pattern of negativity to family planning in the country, despite a high level of literacy, and a culture that appears to operate on the principle of Garrit Hardin's (1968) Law of the Commons, not even powerful edicts from the country's leaders to establish protected areas will have any effect. Protected areas are treated as commons for one to exploit before the next person can; there are numerous protected areas and parks that exist only on paper. Hamann et al. (1999) describe how the North Negros Forest Reserve, which had an original extent of 80,500 hectares, was reduced to about 9,800 hectares at the time of their work in this submontane rainforest. There are many more such examples.

As we attempt here to address the title of the present volume, I am afraid that the ways of life of the Philippine Negrito hunter-gatherers, and other Philippine tribal peoples who depended on these forests, will be totally extinguished well before the end of the twenty-first century, if it has not happened already.

Acknowledgment

Figure 6.3 is reprinted here with permission from the New York Botanical Garden Press. Originally published in B. C. Tan and J. P. Rojo, The Philippines. In D. G. Campbell and H. D. Hammond (eds.), *Floristic Inventory of Tropical Countries*, 44–62, copyright 1989, The New York Botanical Garden.

Estimated % Old Growth Forest Cover in the Philippines over Time

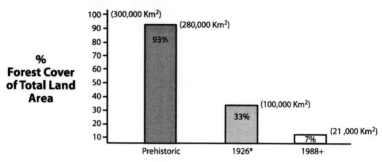

* Merrill, E.D., 1926. Enumeration of Philippine Flowering Plants

+Government of the Philippines, Forest management Bureau (DENR). 1988. Philippine-German Forest Resources Inventory: National Forest Resources of the Philippines.

Figure 6.1. Graphic illustration of forest loss from the prehistoric period through the end of the first quarter of the twentieth century to 1988.

Population Growth and Deforestation on Negros Island, Philippines

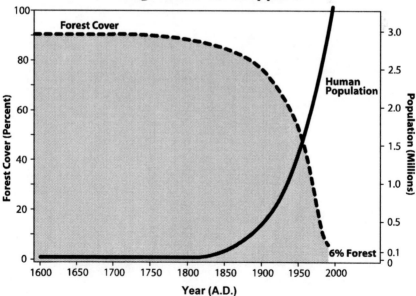

Figure. 6.2. Relationship of human population growth and the decline of forest cover on Negros Island, from Heaney and Regelado (1998).

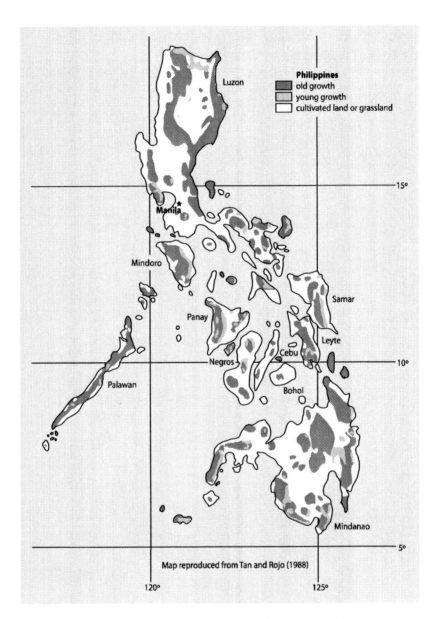

Figure 6.3. A visual representation of remaining forest in the Philippines
    according to Tan and Rojo (1988).

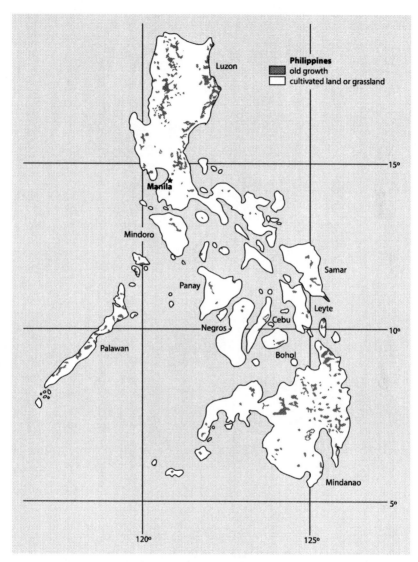

Figure 6.4. An alternative representation of actual extent of old-growth forest in 1988, based on the work of the Philippine-German Forest Resources Inventory (Government of the Philippines, 1988).

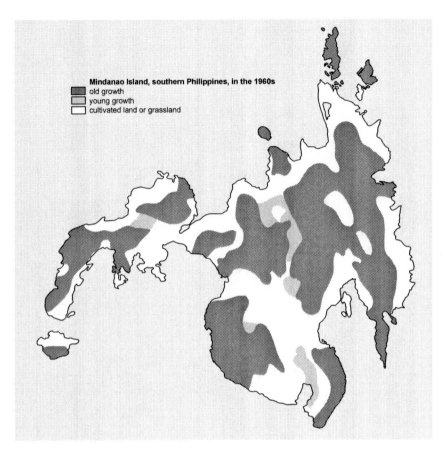

Figure 6.5. Forest cover on Mindanao in the 1960s. Based on maps produced at the Manila Observatory under the direction of Father Peter Walpole.

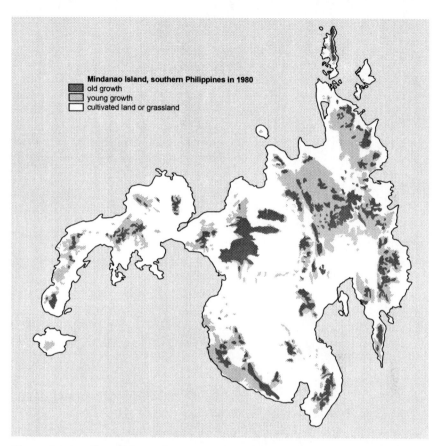

Figure 6.6. Decline of forest cover on Mindanao from the 1960s to 1980. Based on maps produced at the Manila Observatory under the direction of Father Peter Walpole.

References Cited

Cruz, Maria Concepcion J. 2000. Population Pressure, Poverty, and Deforestation: Philippines Case Study. Paper presented at the Asian Population Network Workshop on Population and Environment: Methods of Analysis, Penang, Malaysia, April 10–11.

Government of the Philippines, Forest management Bureau (DENR). 1988. *Philippine-German Forest Resources Inventory.* National Forest Resources of the Philippines.

Hamann, A., E. B. Barbon, E. Curio, and D. A. Madulid. 1999. A Botanical Inventory of a Submontane Tropical Rainforest on Negros Island, Philippines. *Biodiversity & Conservation* 8:1017–1031.

Hardin, Garritt. 1968. The Tragedy of the Commons. *Science* 162:1243–1248.

Heaney, L. R., and J. C. Regelado. 1998. *Vanishing Treasures of the Philippine Rain Forest.* Chicago, Ill.: The Field Museum.

Koopowitz, H., S. H. Sohmer, A. Thornhill, and G. Perez. 1998. Deforestation and Plant Species Extinctions in the Philippines: *Psychotria* as an Example. In C. I. Peng and P. P. Lowry (eds.), *Rare, Threatened, and Endangered Floras of Asia and the Pacific Rim Monograph Series* 16:111–121. Taiwan: Institute of Botany, Academia Sinica.

Mattoon, A. T. 1998. Paper Forests. *World Watch,* 20–28 (March/April).

Merrill, E. D. 1922–1926. *An Enumeration of Philippine Flowering Plants.* Vols. 1–4. Manila: Bureau of Printing.

Sohmer, S. H. unpublished. The genus *Psychotria* (Rubiaceae) in the Philippine Archipelago.

Tan B. C., and J. P. Rojo. 1988. The Philippines. In D. G. Campbell and H. D. Hammond (eds.), *Floristic Inventory of Tropical Countries: The Status of Plant Systematics, Collections, and Vegetation, plus Recommendations for the Future,* 46–62. New York: New York Botanical Garden.

Chapter 7

Tropical Deforestation and Culture Change among the Agta of the Sierra Madre, Eastern Luzon: A Photographic Depiction

Thomas N. Headland

The Agta Negritos of eastern Luzon underwent traumatic cultural change in the twentieth century as a result of deforestation—among other acculturative forces. Other chapters in this volume describe this change. This chapter illustrates some of those changes through a series of photographs. Shown here first are some early photos that the Headlands took in northern Aurora Province in the 1960s and 1970s, and that Bion Griffin took in the 1980s. Following those are some photos taken by John D. Early and T. Headland during their fieldwork in northern Aurora in 1994 after the Agta had changed from foragers to peasants.

When Janet and Tom Headland began their fieldwork among the Agta in 1962, the Sierra Madre forest was 80% old-growth full-closure forest and the Agta were still living a foraging lifestyle with symbiotic trade relationships with non-Agta farmers in the lowland valleys. (See figure 7.2.)

By the 1990s, only 3% of the old-growth forest remained, and the Agta culture and economy had changed drastically from one of foraging to a peasant lifestyle. Today, 2002, the Agta are surrounded by many thousands of Filipino homesteaders who have entered the Agta lands, cut down the forest, and who now outnumber the Agta in northern Aurora by a ratio of 85 to 1.

J. Early and T. Headland (1998) have divided twentieth century Casiguran Agta history into three periods. These were (1) the *Forager Phase* up to 1964 when the Agta were still able to live their traditional hunter-gatherer lifestyle based on collecting and trading forest products with downriver farmers for rice. (See figure 7.3.) (2) The second period, the *Transition Phase,* was from 1965 to 1979, when the Agta slowly moved from their foraging economy toward a livelihood based on wage labor as their forest resources declined. (3) Finally, the third period, the *Peasant Phase,* is dated from 1980 to the end of the century, as the Agta slowly moved towards peasantization when Filipino colonists moved into their forestlands, loggers destroyed the forest, and ecological degradation overcame the region. The photographs in this chapter attempt to illustrate some of the changes that came with these three phases.

Characteristics of Agta Life during the Forager Phase

When the Headlands first began living with the Agta near the end of their Forager Phase in 1962, most Agta did not know they lived in the Philippines, they were preliterate, and few could understand Tagalog, the national language (Headland 1975). They did not then wear Western clothing, and they practiced a nomadic lifestyle living together in small kin-related camp groups that moved several times a year. Men always carried bows and arrows, and women made woven baskets. Families of four or five slept on the ground in lean-to shelters or in tiny huts with bamboo floors that averaged in floor area only 3.9 square meters (4.7 sq. yards) (figures 7.6 and 7.7). In the 1960s Agta still had wild meat to eat on a daily basis: deer, wild pig, monkey, or fish, and sometimes python (see figures 7.8 and 7.9). They lived separately from lowland Filipinos, with the forest areas to themselves, where they sometimes cultivated small gardens. They practiced a traditional animistic religion, with 13% of the adults being spirit mediums (shamans) (Headland 1987). They used traditional plant medicines, and called on their shamans to conduct séances for more serious illnesses.

Characteristics of Agta Life in the Peasant Phase

By the end of the twentieth century, all of this had changed. Today the Agta are well-versed in national politics, vote in elections, and make trips by bus to Manila. Today at least 15% of those aged fifteen to thirty can read in both their own language and in Tagalog; all now wear commercially manufactured clothing. (The Headlands saw only one older man wearing a G-string in 2002.) They no longer file their teeth, wear earplugs, or scarify their bodies, and only the older people still wear armbands. They still live in small houses, but their settlements are now sedentary (no longer temporary "camps"), and houses have outside walls often made of boards—scrap lumber from the logging companies—rather than palm leaves. No women weave baskets today. Instead, containers in their houses consist of plastic buckets, cardboard cartons, and cellophane bags. Families now have many commercially bought goods such as matches, powdered soap, kerosene, sugar, coffee, canned mackerel, flashlights, radios, etc., and in some settlements even a chain saw. Bows and arrows are no longer seen, and young men today know neither how to make or shoot a bow and arrow, although they are skilled at playing basketball on cement courts in nearby lowlander settlements (figures 7.13 and 7.14). With the deer extinct and the wild pigs, monkeys, and fish almost gone, the Agta today get most of their protein from cheap canned fish they buy in town, or from snails the children gather on the coral reefs. And a most salient characteristic, the one that moves them from being independent foragers into a new societal type—namely peasants—is their dependence on the national economy for their livelihood and their lower class status as landless agricultural laborers to the non-Negrito Filipino farmers and merchants (figures 7.20, 7.21). Another main catalyst that brought change to northern Aurora was when the first government road was made into Casiguran in 1977 (but not fully completed until the mid-1980s). The road opened the way for many thousands of Filipinos to migrate into northern Aurora, and brought the whole area, including the Agta, into a market and cash economy (figure 7.15).

The Effect of the Philippine Timber Industry

While the opening of the road into northern Aurora was a major force for the ecological and cultural changes in the area, the primary agent for change was the logging industry. There were a few small logging enterprises in the Casiguran area before the Headlands arrived in 1962.

The first commercial logging operations in the area began in 1928 with the establishment of a sawmill seven kilometers west of the town of Casiguran. This was the Philippine Lumber Exportation Company, managed by two Japanese managers. It functioned until the outbreak of World War Two. There was another logging company managed by some Spaniards on the upper peninsula of Casiguran from 1949 to 1951, and right after that a Chinese-managed logging company opened a logging camp on the lower peninsula for three years in the 1950s.

However, logging did not become a major industry in northern Aurora until the 1960s. Beginning then, the industry invaded Aurora Province and this continued up to the end of the twentieth century.[1] By the end of the 1970s there were reported to be "close to 10,000 persons...engaged in logging [in all of Aurora, not just Casiguran], and more than 40 [logging] firms operating [in the Province]" (Parumog 1982:4).

There were four logging companies working the Casiguran Sierra Madre area at this time: Casiguran Bay Timber Corporation, Industries Development Corporation, RCC Timber Company, and Pacific Timber Export Corporation (popularly known as PATECO). Figure 7.16 gives the reader an idea of the immensity of these logging establishments. During their tenure, the Headlands visited all of these companies on numerous occasions. The main logging camps were much more modernized than the three municipal towns in northern Aurora. In 1969 the camp at Lawang, six kilometers northwest of Casiguran, had 24-hour electricity, running water, flush toilets, their own medical doctor, private airplane service, and of course their own jeeps and trucks. In some logging camps in the early 1970s the managers' offices were air-conditioned and guests were served Magnolia ice cream flown in from Manila. The Acoje Mining camp north of Casiguran flew in supplies weekly during the 1960s in DC3 twin-engine aircraft.

---

[1] The Headlands did not see any active logging on their last field trip to northern Aurora in early 2002.

The destruction of the Agta's rainforest homelands during the Headlands' forty-year tenure there was shocking. (See Headland 1988 and see figure 7.18.) The history of logging and industrial mining in northern Aurora is reviewed in detail in Headland (1986:250–256) and in Early and Headland (1998:26–43). (See also figures 7.17 and 7.19.) It should not be hard for the reader to imagine the effect this had on the Agta as their forest and virtually all of their important traditional resources were destroyed during the last half of the 1900s. The depletion of the closed-canopy forest, as well as game and aquatic life, destroyed the ecological base of the Agta foraging way of life. It was these kinds of changes that forced the Agta themselves to change from foragers to a peasantized post-foraging society by the beginning of the third millennium.

No longer living separated from lowland homesteads, all Agta now live within just a few minutes' walk of non-Agta lowlander farmers, and they are today outnumbered by lowland Filipinos twelve to one in remote areas and by 85 to one in the overall area of northern Aurora. While a few isolated families in the mountains may still practice the old healing rituals and séances, all Agta today use Western medicines such as aspirin for minor illnesses, and go to the town hospital for serious cases, rather than relying on traditional shamanistic folk healers (figure 7.12). And beginning in the 1990s, many Agta have converted to Christianity (M. Griffin 1996). By the end of the 1980s all Agta had become incorporated into the rural labor market, which is what defines them as peasants today (P. B. Griffin 1994; Early and Headland 1998:50–53).

Finally, one salient social change is the recent pattern of exogamous marriages of Agta women to lowlander men. Until the 1980s, almost all Agta marriages were to other Agta. Since the mid-1980s, hypergynous marriages (Agta women marrying non-Agta men) have become common, to the point where 40% of the new marriages of Casiguran Agta women in the last fifteen years have been hypergynous (Headland and Headland 1998). All of these women migrated out of the Agta population when they married lowlanders, and the mixed-blood children of most of these interethnic unions do not speak Agta as their mother tongue (figure 7.23).

Culture Change Is Not Always Bad

Not all of these changes are bad. For example, the Agta praise the government hospital in Casiguran, which they recognize has saved many more Agta lives than did their traditional ritual cures (figure 7.22). And all older Agta we have interviewed claim they prefer their way of life today over their traditional past lifestyle. They not only value modern medicines, but they welcome the cash economy and the opportunity to do casual labor for new in-migrant lowlanders today over their past symbiotic trade relationships with farmers. That is because they get paid in cash (the equivalent of U.S. $2.50 a day), worth almost triple (in buying power) what they could earn in the 1960s.

Still, not all of the changes are good, either. The introduction of commercial liquor has turned at least half of Agta adults into chronic alcoholics. Western-educated outsiders would be appalled at the deforestation of the Sierra Madre over the last quarter century, and the destruction of almost all of the coral reefs both from commercial dynamite fishing during the same period and from silt from deforested hillsides that suffocates the living coral (figure 7.18).[2] The traditional Agta music (sung on a three-tone scale) is never heard today. Instead, Agta young people croon Tagalog love songs they learn by listening to radios. Perhaps the only way one can hear Agta music today is to listen to what the Headlands recorded in the 1960s, now posted on the Internet (http://www.sil.org/imc/agta.htm).[3] A very negative aspect of all this change is manifested in the Agta's loss of their land rights and their human rights. Those deplorable aspects of Agta cultural change are already discussed in chapters 4 and 5 of this volume, and need not be repeated here.

The following photographs depict some of the above-described changes. The first set of photos (figures 7.1 to 7.13) illustrates how most Agta were living when they were still foragers in Casiguran. The second set of photos (figures 7.14 to 7.23) shows how the Agta have changed in the Peasant Phase of their history and especially today as they enter into the third millennium. Each photo caption identifies the photographer and the year the photograph was taken.

---

[2] Other changes among the Agta are startling to observe. The Casiguran Agta language is clearly an Endangered Language today, and will almost surely go extinct, along with the Agta traditional culture, well before the end of the twenty-first century. Another symptom of how the Agta are changing is that in March 2002, when the Headlands returned to Manila after a field visit in Casiguran, they received cell-phone calls from Agta living in Manila virtually every day for ten days. They had never before talked on a telephone with an Agta, not even when they made their last previous trip to the Agta in 2000.

[3] To find out more about Agta music, see "Addendum 1: Archival Sources of Agta Music" in the "Bibliography of the Agta of Eastern Luzon," chapter 8 of this volume.

Photographs of the Agta When They Were Still Foragers

Figure 7.1. Agta man, showing how men dressed and carried bow and arrows wherever they went during their "Forager Phase." (Janet Headland, 1962)

Figure 7.2. A lowlander couple visits their Agta trading partners in a forest camp. The mortar lying on its side was made by Agta, used to pound unhusked rice grain. (B. Griffin, 1981 or 1982)

Figure 7.3. Agta woman pounding rice to remove the husk. For centuries Agta have exchanged forest products (often wild meat) with lowland farmers for rice, corn, or root crops. Today they are paid in cash when they do service tasks or agricultural labor for lowlanders. (T. Headland, 1970)

Figure 7.4. A group of boys posing in front of an Agta camp on a forest riverbed. (T. Headland, 1962)

Figure 7.5. Agta man weaving a fish trap of bamboo and rattan. He is sitting next to a wooden rice mortar. His partially-finished house is behind him. (Janet Headland, 1966)

Figure 7.6. An Agta camp group in their lean-to shelters on the beach (T. Headland, 1962)

Figure 7.7. A traditional Agta rainy-season house, with man carrying bamboo water container. (T. Headland, 1962)

Figure 7.8. A freshly killed python *(Python reticulatus)* being held by two Agta men. It measured 22 feet 10 inches long, with a circumference of 26 inches. (Janet Headland, 1970)

Figure 7.9. The fresh skin of the python shown in the previous photo. The man
in straw hat killed this snake on June 9, 1970, with a shotgun. Headland
stands at far left. The Headlands' oldest daughter, Rachel, is in the middle.
Agta eat the meat of pythons but not of other species of snake.
(Janet Headland, 1970)

Figure 7.10. Agta hunter carrying a freshly killed wild pig. (T. Headland, 1962)

Figure 7.11. Agta family preparing to butcher a monkey by first burning off the hair. (Janet Headland, 1963)

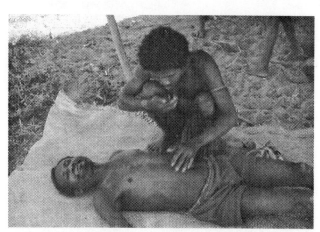

Figure 7.12. An Agta shaman (spirit medium) spits betel quid on his hand and smears it on the belly and upper body of a sick man. The shaman is in a trance, chanting and possessed by his spirit friend. The patient recovered. (T. Headland, 1976)

Figure 7.13. Until the 1970s, all Agta boys knew how to shoot small bows and arrows by the time they were four, and by age ten they often came home with small birds they had shot in the nearby forest. These children would typically pluck and clean their birds (often just one tiny sparrow), roast the meat on coals, and then divide up and distribute small portions to their playmates. This child (here age 3) is the son of Eleden Aduanan, the man to whom this book is dedicated. (T. Headland, 1963)

Photographs of the Agta as They Became Peasants

Figure 7.14. A group of Agta teenage boys, playing basketball, in 1994. In contrast to the three-year-old Agta boy in figure 7.13, these teenagers have probably never shot a bow and arrow or killed a deer or wild pig. But they are as skilled at shooting baskets today as boys were with their bows in the 1960s. Note the photo background; once dense forest, it is now completely deforested, including the mountains on the San Ildefonso Peninsula in the far background. (J. Early, 1994)

Figure 7.15. The government road into northern Aurora, built in 1977 and made operational in the mid-1980s. The section of the road shown here is just three kilometers south of Casiguran town. The two buildings on the far side of the road are the Casiguran hospital, also built in the late 1970s and made operational in the mid-1980s. The doctors and nurses at this hospital have saved many Agta lives. (T. Headland, 1994)

Figure 7.16. The PATECO logging company at Dilasag, Casiguran, in northern
    Aurora in the 1980s. (B. Griffin, 1986). The logging industry is arguably the
    major catalyst for the ecological changes in the Sierra Madre, and thus
    indirectly the primary cause of Agta culture change.

Figure 7.17. A logging truck passing through an Agta settlement.
    (J. Early, 1994)

Figure 7.18. The Kinabunglan rivershed, in February 1994, after a logging
    company had spent a month cutting trees there. The loggers used nine
    bulldozers and about twenty trucks to haul the logs. The next heavy rain
    brought numerous landslides, destroying much of the resources of this area,
    where the Kinabunglan Agta band have lived for centuries. The silt from the
    rain-flooded Kinabunglan River spread out for miles in the Casiguran Bay,
    killing some of the coral reefs adjacent to the mouth of the river. (Aerial
    photo by J. Early, 1994)

Figure 7.19. An Agta woman asks for some diesel fuel from loggers as they pass
    her house in a bulldozer. (J. Early, 1994)

Figure 7.20. An Agta family today works for a non-Agta farmer at husking coconuts to make copra, for which they will receive a share of the profit when the copra is sold in the market. (Janet Headland, 1986)

Figure 7.21. An Agta laborer harvesting rice for a lowland farmer. (T. Headland, 1994)

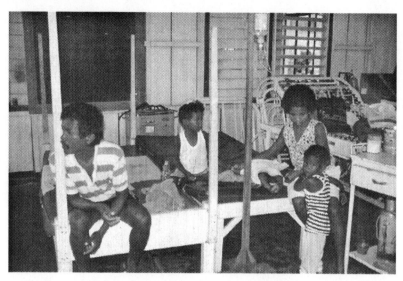

Figure 7.22. An Agta couple with three of their children. Two of the children, ill with pneumonia, were inpatients at the Casiguran hospital, where their lives were saved with antibiotics. (J. Early, 1994)

Figure 7.23. A hypergynous marriage—an Agta woman and her lowlander husband, with three of their five living half-blood children. Between 1985 and 2000, 40% of Casiguran Agta women who married were married to lowland farmer men, and in every case those women migrated out of the Agta population when they married. (J. Early, 1994)

References Cited

Early, John D., and Thomas N. Headland. 1998. *Population Dynamics of a Philippine Rain Forest People: The San Ildefonso Agta.* Gainesville: University Press of Florida.

Griffin, Marcus B. 1996. Jesus among the Trees: Deforestation, Biodiversity Conservation, and the Adoption of Christianity among the Palanan Agta. Paper presented at the 95th Annual Meeting of the American Anthropological Association, San Francisco, November 20–24.

Griffin, P. Bion. 1994. Becoming Filipino Peasants: Agta Forager Gender Role Changes. In Linda J. Ellanna (ed.), *Hunters and Gatherers In the Modern Context: Book of Presented Papers* 1:234–238. Fairbanks: University of Alaska.

Headland, Thomas N. 1975. Report of Eastern Luzon Language Survey. *Philippine Journal of Linguistics* 6:47–54.

Headland, Thomas N. 1986. *Why Foragers Do Not Become Farmers: A Historical Study of a Changing Ecosystem and Its Effect on a Negrito Hunter-Gatherer Group in the Philippines.* Ann Arbor, Mich.: University Microfilms International. [Abstract in *Dissertation Abstracts International* 47(6), 1986.]

Headland, Thomas N. 1987. Negrito Religions: Negritos of the Philippine Islands. In Mircea Eliade (ed.), *The Encyclopedia of Religion* 10:348–349. New York: Macmillan.

Headland, Thomas N. 1988. Ecosystemic Change in a Philippine Tropical Rain Forest and its Effect on a Negrito Foraging Society. *Tropical Ecology* 29(2):121–135.

Headland, Thomas N., and Janet D. Headland. 1998. Hypergyny: The Outmarriages of Agta Women and the Future of Philippine Negrito Post-Foraging Populations. Paper presented at the 97th Annual Meeting of the American Anthropological Association, Philadelphia, PA, December 2–6.

Parumog, Benedicto P. 1982. Schedule for Market Values 1981–1982 for the Province of Aurora. [Bound typescript, 137 pages, on file at the Casiguran Municipal Hall in 1985.]

Chapter 8

A Bibliography of
the Agta of Eastern Luzon, Philippines

Thomas N. Headland and P. Bion Griffin, compilers

In the Philippines there are thirty-three known language groups of "Negritos," the aboriginal peoples of that island nation. These Negritos, found on several islands, number in total about 33,000. (See table 4.1 in chapter 4 of this volume.) All of these groups are classed as hunter-gatherers or, more correctly today, as post-foraging societies. Fifteen of these groups are found today scattered throughout the Sierra Madre mountain range and coastal beaches along the eastern coast of Luzon in the largest area of rainforest in the Philippines. These fifteen groups call themselves and their languages *Agta.* (Three of the Agta groups use the cognate terms *Alta* or *Arta.*) They number together about 11,000 people.

This updated bibliography (to the year 2001) includes every publicly available reference known to the compilers that would be of academic interest to students of Negrito societies. This is the third edition of the bibliography. The first edition was published eighteen years ago (see Griffin and Headland 1985), and the second edition on the Internet five years ago (Headland and Griffin 1997). References below include unpublished papers presented at national or international conferences only if formal copies of those papers were distributed at the conference and are in the possession of the compilers. This present updated bibliography includes 176 references on the Agta groups. It is followed at the end by a short addendum of archival sources of Agta music and a second short addendum listing eight important bibliographic resources on Philippine Negritos in general.

Abate, Tom. 1992. Into the Northern Philippines Rainforest. *BioScience* 42 (4):246–251 (April).

Aduanan, Pompoek, and Thomas N. Headland. 1991. How Juan Got His Wife From Above [Analysis of an Agta Folktale]. In Hazel J. Wrigglesworth (ed.), *The Maiden of Many Nations: The Skymaiden Who Married a Man from Earth*, 211–215. Manila: Linguistic Society of the Philippines.

Allen, Melinda S. 1985. The Rain Forest of Northeast Luzon and Agta Foragers. In P. Bion Griffin and Agnes Estioko-Griffin (eds.), *The Agta of Northeastern Luzon: Recent Studies*, 45–68. Cebu City, Philippines: University of San Carlos Publications.

Amazona, D. 1951. Some Customs of the Aetas of the Baler Area, Philippines. *Primitive Man* 24:21–34.

Baer, G. A. 1907. Contribution a L'etude des Langues des Indigenes aux Iles Philippines. *Anthropos* 2:467–491. [Includes word lists of 100 words of twenty-two Philippine dialects, nine of which are Negrito languages, includeing Casiguran Agta and "Palauan" [sic. Palanan] Agta.]

Barbosa, Artemio. 1985. The Ethnography of the Agta of Lamika, Penablanca, Cagayan. In P. Bion Griffin and Agnes Estioko-Griffin (eds.), *The Agta of Northeastern Luzon: Recent Studies*, 12–17. Cebu City, Philippines: University of San Carlos Publications.

Benedicto, Lourdes C. 1977. Blackboard Newspaper and the Dumagats of Calabgan, Casiguran, Quezon. M.A. thesis in Journalism. University of the Philippines, Diliman.

Bennagen, Ponciano L. 1969. Becoming an Anthropologist: Fieldwork among the Agta of Palanan, Isabela. In M. Zamora (ed.), *Anthropology: Range and Relevance*, 184–191. Quezon City: Kayumanggi Publishers.

Bennagen, Ponciano L. 1969. The Agta of Palanan, Isabela: Surviving Food-Gatherers, Hunters and Fisherman. *Esso Silangan* 14(3):5–7.

Bennagen, Ponciano L. 1976. Kultura at Kapaligiran: Pangkulturang Pagbabago at Kapanatagan ng mga Agta sa Palanan, Isabela. M.A. thesis. Department of Anthropology, University of the Philippines, Diliman. [Written in Tagalog.]

Bennagen, Ponciano L. 1977. Pagbabago at Pag-unlad ng mga Agta sa Palanan, Isabela. *Diwa* 6(1–4):1–103. [Written in Tagalog.]

Bennagen, Ponciano L. 1977. Societal Responses to Environmental Problems: Subsistence, Settlement and Community Patterning among the Agta of Palanan, Isabela. Paper presented at the Twelfth American Studies Seminar, Laguna, October 24–29.

Bennagen, Ponciano L. 1977. The Negrito: A Rallying Call to Save a Filipino Group from Cultural Extinction. In *Filipino Heritage: The Making of a Nation*. Manila: Lahing Pilipino Publishing Co.

Bennagen, Ponciano. 1985. Philippines: Swidden Cultivation among the Dumagat [Agta]. In *Swidden Cultivation in Asia,* Vol. 3 [No editor given.], 213–295. Bangkok: Unesco Regional Office.

Blumentritt, F. 1883. On the East Coast of Luzon, After G. Wallis' Diary. *Globus* 46:377ff. [On the Negritos near Binangonan.]

Blumentritt, F. 1884. Die Negritos von Baler. *Mitteilungen der Kaiserlich-koniglichen Geographischen Gesellschaft in Wien* 27:317–321.

Blumentritt, F. 1884. Gaddanen, Ilongoten, Ibilaos and Negritos des Valley de Cagayan (Luzon). *Boletin de la Sociedad Anthropologica de Viena* 14.

Blumentritt, F. 1896. P. Castano's Nachrichten uber Bikols, Cimarronen, und Agtas. *Mitteilungen der Kaiserlich-koniglichen Geographischen Gesellschaft in Wien* 39:300–310.

Blumentritt, Ferdinand. 1896. Des Padre Fr. Jose Castano Nachrichten uber die Sprache der Agta (Philippinen). *Bijdragen tot de taal-land-en volkendunde* 46:434–436.

Castano, P. 1895. Noticia del Vicol. In W. Retana (ed.), *Archivo del Bibliofilo Filipino,* Vol. 1. [Does not indicate number of pages.]

Clark, Constance D. 1990. The Trading Networks of the Northeastern Cagayan Agta Negritos. M.A. thesis in Anthropology. University of Hawai'i.

Conservation International. 1991. Last Wilderness in the Philippines under Threat. *Tropicus* [a quarterly report to members of Conservation International] 4(3):1, 6–7 (Fall).

Conservation International. 1991. *The Palanan Wilderness.* Washington D.C.: Conservation International. [A 12-page report in booklet form with color photos of Conservation International's 1991 biological diversity survey of Palanan, Isabela.]

Constantino, Ernesto, ed. 2001. *Nanang: I Taguwasi anna I Innawagan* (Epic: Taguwasi and Innawagan) (An Agta Negrito Epic Chanted by Baket Anag). ELPR Publications Series A3-003. Osaka, Japan: Endangered Languages of the Pacific Rim, Osaka Gakuin University. [Preface and Introduction in English, 8 pages; Epic text in Central Cagayan Agta language with English translation, pp. 1–26; ISSN 1346-082X. For information contact ELPR Project Director Osahito Miyaoka at email elpr@utc.osaka-gu.ac.jp.]

Early, John D., and Thomas N. Headland. 1998. *Population Dynamics of a Philippine Rain Forest People: The San Ildefonso Agta.* Gainesville: University Press of Florida.

Estioko-Griffin, Agnes A. 1984. The Ethnography of Southeastern Cagayan Agta Hunting. M.A. thesis in Anthropology. University of the Philippines.

Estioko-Griffin, Agnes A. 1985. Women as Hunters: The Case of an Eastern Cagayan Agta Group. In P. Bion Griffin and Agnes A. Estioko-Griffin (eds.), *The Agta of Northeastern Luzon: Recent Studies,* 18–32. Cebu City, Philippines: University of San Carlos Publications.

Estioko-Griffin, Agnes A. 1986. Daughters of the Forest. *Natural History* 95(5):36–43 (May). [Reprinted 1987 In Phillip Whitten and David E. Hunter (eds.), *Anthropology: Contemporary Perspectives,* 5th ed., 234–237. Boston: Little, Brown and Co.]

Estioko-Griffin, Agnes A., and P. Bion Griffin. 1975. The Ebuked Agta of Northeastern Luzon. *Philippine Quarterly of Culture and Society* 3:237–244.

Estioko-Griffin, Agnes A., and P. Bion Griffin. 1981. The Beginnings of Cultivation among the Agta Hunter-Gatherers in Northeastern Luzon. In Harold Olofson (ed.), *Adaptive Strategies and Change in Philippine Swidden-based Societies,* 55–72. Laguna, Philippines: Forest Research Institute.

Estioko-Griffin, Agnes A., and P. Bion Griffin. 1981. Woman the Hunter: The Agta. In Frances Dahlberg (ed.), *Woman the Gatherer,* 121–151. New Haven: Yale University Press.

Estioko-Griffin, Agnes A., and P. Bion Griffin. 1984. Women Hunters: The Implications for Pleistocene Prehistory and Contemporary Ethnography. In Madeleine J. Goodman (ed.), *Women in Asia and the Pacific: Toward an East-West Dialogue,* 61–81. Honolulu: University of Hawai'i.

Evrard, Alain. 1979. Encounter with a Vanishing Forest People: The Pugot [Agta] of Isabela. *Orientations* 10(11):34–39 (November). [Published in Hong Kong.]

Goodman, Madeleine J., Agnes A. Estioko-Griffin, and John S. Grove. 1985. Menarche, Pregnancy, Birth Spacing and Menopause among the Agta Women Foragers of Northeastern Luzon, the Philippines. In P. Bion Griffin and Agnes A. Estioko-Griffin (eds.), *The Agta of Northeastern Luzon: Recent Studies,* 147–157. Cebu City, Philippines: University of San Carlos Publications.

Goodman, Madeleine J., P. Bion Griffin, Agnes A. Estioko-Griffin, and John S. Grove. 1985. The Compatibility of Hunting and Mothering among the Agta Hunter-Gatherers of the Philippines. *Sex Roles* 12:1199–1209.

Griffin, Marcus B. 1994. Return to Palanan. *Mabuhay: Inflight Magazine of Philippine Airlines* 15(3):26–31. (March).

Griffin, Marcus B. 1994. Shifting Political Economy and the Breakdown of Conflict Resolution. In Linda J. Ellanna (ed.), *Hunters and Gatherers in the Modern Context,* Vol. 1, 225–233. Fairbanks: University of Alaska.

Griffin, Marcus B. 1995. Katalakai. *Mabuhay: Inflight magazine of Philippine Airlines* 16(4):18–22 (April).

Griffin, Marcus B. 1996. Change and Stability: Agta Kinship in a History of Uncertainty. Ph.D. dissertation. University of Illinois at Urbana-Champaign. 257 pp. Ann Arbor: University Microfilms International [order no. 9712289].

Griffin, Marcus B. 1996. Jesus among the Trees: Deforestation, Biodiversity Conservation, and the Adoption of Christianity among the Palanan Agta. Paper presented at the 95th Annual Meeting of the American Anthropological Association, San Francisco, November 20–24.

Griffin, Marcus B. 1996. The Cultural Identity of Foragers and the Agta of Palanan, Isabela, the Philippines. *Anthropos* 91:111–123.

Griffin, Marcus B. 2000. Homicide and Aggression among the Agta of Eastern Luzon, the Philippines, 1910–1985. In Peter P. Schweitzer, Megan Biesele, and Robert K. Hitchcock (eds.), *Hunters and Gatherers in the Modern World*, 94–109. New York: Berghahn Books.

Griffin, Marcus B., and P. Bion Griffin. 1997. Agta Foragers: Alternative Histories, and Cultural Autonomy in Luzon. *The Australian Journal of Anthropology* 8:259–269.

Griffin, P. Bion. 1981. Northern Luzon Agta Subsistence and Settlement. *Filipinas* 2:26–42.

Griffin, P. Bion. 1984. Agta Forager Women in the Philippines. *Cultural Survival* 8(2):21–23.

Griffin, P. Bion. 1984. Forager Resource and Land Use in the Humid Tropics: The Agta of Northeastern Luzon, the Philippines. In Carmel Schrire (ed.), *Past and Present in Hunter-Gatherer Studies*, 95–121. Orlando, Fla.: Academic Press.

Griffin, P. Bion. 1985. A Contemporary View of the Shift from Hunting to Horticulture: The Agta Case. In V. N. Misra and Peter Bellwood (eds.), *Recent Advances in Indo-Pacific Prehistory*, 349–352. New Delhi: Oxford IBH Publishing.

Griffin, P. Bion. 1985. Luzon Hokutobuno Agtazokuno Seikei Keizaito Shuraku [Agta Living Economics and a Village Structure: The Agta of Northeastern Luzon]. *Etonosu* [*Ethnos* in Asia] 27:5–20, 41–54. [Published in Shimonosekishi City, Japan. Translated from the English by Masao Nishimura.]

Griffin, P. Bion. 1985. Population Movements and Socio-economic Change in the Sierra Madre. In P. Bion Griffin and Agnes A. Estioko-Griffin (eds.), *The Agta of Northeastern Luzon: Recent Studies*, 85–101. Cebu City, Philippines: University of San Carlos Publications.

Griffin, P. Bion. 1985. Ruson-to-Hokutobu-no Seikei-keizai-to Shuraku [Northeastern Luzon Agta Subsistence and Settlement]. *Etonosu* [*Ethnos* in Asia] 27:41–54 with 20 plates. [In Japanese; translated into Japanese by Masao Nishimura.]

Griffin, P. Bion. 1985. *The Agta of the Foragers: Ethnoarchaeology and Ethnography.* Weston, CT: Pictures of Record. [A slide set of 80 slides on the Agta published for educational use; price $114.]

Griffin, P. Bion. 1989. Hunting, Farming, and Sedentism in a Rain Forest Foraging Society. In Susan Kent (ed.), *Farmers as Hunters: The Implications of Sedentism*, 60–70. Cambridge: Cambridge University Press.

Griffin, P. Bion. 1991. Philippine Agta Forager-Serfs: Commodities and Exploitation. *Senri Ethnological Papers* 30:199–222.

Griffin, P. Bion. 1994. Becoming Filipino Peasants: Agta Forager Gender Role Changes. In Linda J. Ellanna (ed.), *Hunters and Gatherers in the Modern Context: Book of Presented Papers,* Vol. 1, 234–238. Fairbanks, University of Alaska.

Griffin, P. Bion. 1997. Technology and Variation in Arrow Design among the Agta of Northeastern Luzon. In Heidi Knecht (ed.), *Projectile Technology,* 267–286. New York: Plenum.

Griffin, P. Bion. 1998. An Ethnographic View of the Pig in Selected Traditional Southeast Asian Societies. *MASCA Research Papers in Science and Archaeology* 15:27–37.

Griffin, P. Bion, and Agnes A. Estioko-Griffin, eds. 1985. *The Agta of Northeastern Luzon: Recent Studies.* Cebu City, Philippines: University of San Carlos Publications. [Includes 188 pp.; 12 chapters by 10 authors, 14 photos, and index.]

Griffin, P. Bion, and Agnes A. Estioko-Griffin. 1978. Ethnoarchaeology of Agta Hunter-Gatherers. *Archaeology* 31(6):34–43.

Griffin, P. Bion, and Agnes A. Estioko-Griffin. 1986. Maipaspasuli kadi lattan ti Aeta? *Bannawag* [Philippine magazine] February 10:5, 32–34. [Written in Ilokano.]

Griffin, P. Bion, and Marcus B. Griffin. 1992. Fathers and Childcare among the Cagayan Agta. In Barry S. Hewlett (ed.), *Father-Child Relations: Cultural and Biosocial Contexts,* 297–320. Hawthorne, N.Y.: Aldine de Gruyter.

Griffin, P. Bion, and Marcus B. Griffin. 1999. The Agta of Eastern Luzon, Philippines. In Richard B. Lee and Richard Daly (eds.), *The Cambridge Encyclopedia of Hunters and Gatherers,* 289–293. Cambridge: Cambridge University Press.

Griffin, P. Bion, and Marcus B. Griffin. 2000. Agta Hunting and Resource Sustainability in Northeastern Luzon, Philippines. In John G. Robinson and Elizabeth L. Bennett (eds.), *Hunting for Sustainability in Tropical Forests,* 325–335. New York: Columbia University Press.

Griffin, P. Bion, and Thomas N. Headland. 1985. A Selected Bibliography of the Agta Negritos of Eastern Luzon, Philippines. In P. Bion Griffin and Agnes A. Estioko-Griffin (eds.), *The Agta of Northeastern Luzon: Recent Studies,* 166–175. Cebu City, Philippines: University of San Carlos Publications.

Griffin, P. Bion, and Thomas N. Headland. 1994. The Agta of the Philippines. In Goran Burenhult (general editor), *Traditional Peoples Today,* 72–73. Vol. 5 of *The Illustrated History of Humankind,* New York: HarperCollins.

Griffin, P. Bion, and Thomas N. Headland. 1994. The Negritos: Disappearing Hunter-Gatherers of Southeast Asia. In Goran Burenhult (general editor), *Traditional Peoples Today,* 71. Vol. 5 of *The Illustrated History of Humankind.* New York: HarperCollins.

Griffin, P. Bion, M. Goodman, A. Estioko-Griffin, and J. Grove. 1992. Agta Women Hunters: Subsistence, Child Care and Reproduction. In Peter Bellwood (ed.), *Man and his Culture: A Resurgence,* 173–199. New Delhi: Vedams Books International.

Griffin, P. Bion, and Wilhelm G. Solheim, II. 1988–1989. Ethnoarchaeological Research in Asia. *Asian Perspectives* 28(2):145–162.

Guerrero, Virginia. 1971. Education of the Ilongots and Negritos in the Division of Quezon I. M.A. thesis in Education. Philippine Normal College, Manila.

Hamey, E. T. 1879. Etude Sur un Squelette d'Aeta des Environs de Binangonan. *Nouvelles Archives du Museum d'Histoire Naturelle de Paris* 2:181–212.

Headland, Janet D. 1966. Case-marking Particles in Casiguran Agta. *Philippine Journal for Language Teaching* 4(1–2):58–59.

Headland, Thomas N. 1971. Casiguran Dumagat [Phonological Description and Vocabulary]. In Lawrence A. Reid (ed.), *Philippine Minor Languages: Word Lists and Phonologies,* 9, 45ff. (Oceanic Linguistics Special Publication No. 8) Honolulu: University of Hawai'i Press.

Headland, Thomas N. 1975. Report of Eastern Luzon Language Survey. *Philippine Journal of Linguistics* 6:47–54.

Headland, Thomas N. 1975. The Casiguran Dumagat Today and in 1936. *Philippine Quarterly of Culture and Society* 3:245–257.

Headland, Thomas N. 1977. Teeth Mutilation among the Casiguran Dumagat. *Philippine Quarterly of Culture and Society* 5(1–2):54–64.

Headland, Thomas N. 1978. Cultural Ecology, Ethnicity, and the Negritos of Northeastern Luzon: A Review Article. *Asian Perspectives* 21(1):127–139.

Headland, Thomas N. 1981. Imposed Values and Aid Rejection among Philippine Negritos. Paper presented at the Second International Philippine Studies Conference, Honolulu, June 27–30.

Headland, Thomas N. 1981. Taxonomic Disagreement in a Culturally Salient Domain: Botany Versus Utility in a Philippine Negrito Taxonomic System. M.A. thesis, Department of Anthropology, University of Hawai'i, Honolulu. Ann Arbor Michigan: University Microfilms International.

Headland, Thomas N. 1983. An Ethnobotanical Anomaly: The Dearth of Binomial Specifics in a Folk Taxonomy of a Negrito Hunter-Gatherer Society in the Philippines. *Journal of Ethnobiology* 3:109–120.

Headland, Thomas N. 1984. Agta Negritos of the Philippines. *Cultural Survival Quarterly* 8(3):29–31.

Headland, Thomas N. 1985. Comment [on Brown]. *Current Anthropology* 25 (1):57–58.

Headland, Thomas N. 1985. Imposed Values and Aid Rejection among the Casi-
    guran Agta. In P. Bion Griffin and Agnes A. Estioko-Griffin (eds.), *The
    Agta of Northeastern Luzon: Recent Studies,* 102–118. Cebu City, Philip-
    pines: University of San Carlos Publications.
Headland, Thomas N. 1985. International Economics and Tribal Subsistence: A
    Report of a Microeconomic Study of a Negrito Hunter-gatherer Society in
    the Wake of the Philippine Crisis of 1983. *Philippine Quarterly of Culture
    and Society* 13(3):235–239.
Headland, Thomas N. 1986. *Why Foragers Do Not Become Farmers: A His-
    torical Study of a Changing Ecosystem and Its Effect on a Negrito Hunter-
    Gatherer Group in the Philippines.* Ph.D dissertation. University of
    Hawai'i. Ann Arbor, Mich.: University Microfilms International. [order No.
    DA8622099]. [Abstract appears in *Dissertation Abstracts International*
    47(6), 1986.]
Headland, Thomas N. 1987. Additional Negrito Dialects. In Hyatt Moore (ed.),
    Summer Institute of Linguistics Annual Report [for 1986], 6–7. Dallas:
    International Linguistics Center.
Headland, Thomas N. 1987. Kinship and Social Behavior among Agta Negrito
    Hunter-Gatherers. *Ethnology* 26:261–280.
Headland, Thomas N. 1987. Negrito Religions: Negritos of the Philippine
    Islands. In Mircea Eliade (ed.), *The Encyclopedia of Religion,* Vol. 10, 348–
    349. New York: Macmillan.
Headland, Thomas N. 1987. Report of a Case Study of Population Decline in a
    Philippine Negrito Hunter-Gatherer Society. Paper presented at the 86th
    Annual Meeting of the American Anthropological Association, Chicago.
    November 18–22.
Headland, Thomas N. 1987. The Wild Yam Question: How Well Could Inde-
    pendent Hunter-Gatherers Live in a Tropical Rainforest Ecosystem? *Human
    Ecology* 15:463–491.
Headland, Thomas N. 1988. Ecosystemic Change in a Philippine Tropical Rain-
    forest and Its Effect on a Negrito Foraging Society. *Tropical Ecology*
    29(2):121–135.
Headland, Thomas N. 1988. Introduction to the Symposium 'Deculturation and
    Survival among Southeast Asian Negritos: What Can Be Done'? Paper pre-
    sented at the 12th International Congress of Anthropological and Ethnologi-
    cal Sciences, Zagreb, Yugoslavia, July 24–31.
Headland, Thomas N. 1988. Why Foragers Do Not Become Farmers: The Com-
    petitive Exclusion Principle and the Persistence of the Professional Primi-
    tive. Paper presented at the 12th International Congress of Anthropological
    and Ethnological Sciences, Zagreb, Yugoslavia, July 24–31.
Headland, Thomas N. 1989. Population Decline in a Philippine Negrito Hunter-
    Gatherer Society. *American Journal of Human Biology* 1:59–72.

Headland, Thomas N. 1990. Time Allocation, Demography, and Original Affluence in a Philippine Negrito Hunter-Gatherer Society. In 6th International Conference on Hunting and Gathering Societies: Precirculated Papers and Abstracts, Vol. 1, 427–439. Fairbanks: University of Alaska.

Headland, Thomas N. 1991. How Negrito Foragers Live in a Philippine Rainforest: What They Eat and What They Don't Eat. Paper presented at the International Symposium, Food and Nutrition in the Tropical Forest: Biocultural Interactions and Applications to Development (Sponsored by UNESCO), Paris, France, September 10–13.

Headland, Thomas N. 1991. Three Decades among the Agta: Trials and Advantages of Long-Term Fieldwork with Philippine Hunter-Gatherers. Paper presented at the 90th Annual Meeting of the American Anthropological Association, Chicago, November 20–24.

Headland, Thomas N. 1993. Agta: A Cultural Summary. In Paul Hockings (ed.), *Encyclopedia of World Cultures: East and Southeast Asia,* Vol. 5, 4–6. New Haven: Human Relations Area Files.

Headland, Thomas N. 1993. Negritos, Philippines: A Cultural Summary. In Paul Hockings (ed.), *Encyclopedia of World Cultures,* East and Southeast Asia, Vol. 5, 210–211. New Haven: Human Relations Area Files.

Headland, Thomas N. 1999. Managing the Natural Resources of the Sierra Madre: What Is the Role of the Agta? In Eileen Bernardo and Denyse Snelder (eds.), *Co-Managing the Environment: The Natural Resources of the Sierra Madre Mountain Range,* 67–75. Leiden: Leiden University.

Headland, Thomas N., and P. Bion Griffin. 1997. *A Bibliography of the Agta Negritos of Eastern Luzon, Philippines.* SIL Electronic Working Papers 1997-004. Dallas: Summer Institute of Linguistics.
http://www.sil.org/silewp/1997/004/silewp1997-004.html (June 20, 2002).

Headland, Thomas N., and Janet D. Headland. 1974. *A Dumagat (Casiguran)— English Dictionary.* Canberra: Department of Linguistics, Research School of Pacific Studies, The Australian National University.

Headland, Thomas N., and Janet D. Headland. 1978. *Report of Casiguran Dumagat Literacy Survey.* Microfiche PhP499.213. Manila: Ateneo de Manila Libraries.

Headland, Thomas N., and Janet D. Headland. 1984. Casiguran Dumagat Kinship Terminology. In Richard E. Elkins and Gail R. Hendrickson (eds.), *A Sampling of Philippine Kinship Patterns,* 69–73. Manila: Summer Institute of Linguistics.

Headland, Thomas N., and Janet D. Headland. 1988. Rice Cultivation Practices in a Negrito Foraging Society in Northeastern Luzon, Philippines. *International Rice Research Newsletter* 13(5):38 (October).

Headland, Thomas N., and Janet D. Headland. 1994. Westernization, Deculturation, or Extinction among Agta Negritos? Paper presented at the 7th International Conference on Hunting and Gathering Societies, Moscow, Russia, August 17–23, 1994. Published In Linda J. Ellanna (ed.), *Hunters and Gatherers in the Modern Context: Book of Presented Papers,* Vol. 1, 272–284. Fairbanks, University of Alaska.

Headland, Thomas N., and Janet D. Headland. 1997. Limitation of Human Rights, Land Exclusion, and Tribal Extinction: The Agta Negritos of the Philippines. *Human Organization* 56(1):79–90.

Headland, Thomas N., and Alan Healey. 1974. Grammatical Sketch of Casiguran Dumagat. *Pacific Linguistics* A-43:1–54.

Headland, Thomas N., and Lawrence A. Reid. 1989. Hunter-Gatherers and their Neighbors from Prehistory to the Present. *Current Anthropology* 30:43–66.

Headland, Thomas N., and Lawrence A. Reid. 1991. Holocene Foragers and Interethnic Trade: A Critique of the Myth of Isolated Independent Hunter-Gatherers. In Susan Gregg (ed.), *Between Bands and States: Interaction in Small-Scale Societies,* 333–340. Carbondale: Southern Illinois University.

Headland, Thomas N., and Elmer P. Wolfenden. 1967. The Vowels of Casiguran Dumagat. In Mario D. Zamora (ed.), *Studies in Philippine Anthropology,* 592–596. Quezon City: Amelia-Phoenix.

Healey, Phyllis M. 1958. An Agta Conversation Text. *Oceanic Linguistic Monographs* 3:65–72.

Healey, Phyllis M. 1960. *An Agta Grammar.* Manila: Bureau of Printing.

Howell, Nancy. 1999. The Demographic Puzzle of the Philippine Agta. [A review article]. *Current Anthropology* 40:405–406.

Hutterer, Karl L. 1978. Dean C. Worcester and Philippine Anthropology. *Philippine Quarterly of Culture and Society* 6(3):125–156.

Keesing, Felix. 1962. *The Ethnohistory of Northern Luzon.* Stanford, Calif.: Stanford University Press.

Kern, [Hendrik]. 1896. Opmerkingen omtrent de taal der Agta's van 't Schiereiland Camarines (Filippijnen). *Bijdragen tot de taal- land- en volkenkunde* 46:437–440. Reprinted in *Verspreide Geschriften* 11:78–82.

Lindbergh, Charles A. 1972. Lessons from the Primitive. *Reader's Digest* 101:147–151.

Lukban, Vicente. 1914. Report del Gobernador de Tayabas Hon. Vicente Luckban [sic] al Secretario del Interior Hon. Winfred T. Denison Sobre la Cuestion de los Tribus Infieles en Dicha Provincia. In H. Otley Beyer (comp.), *Ethnography of the Negrito-Aeta Peoples,* 1918, Vol. 2, Paper No. 50. Typescript, 13 pages. Manila. (A microfilm collection of original sources.) Harvard University Microfilm Dept. Harvard Order No. 65-60-38.

Lynch, Frank. 1984. Some Notes on a Brief Survey of the Hill People of Mt. Iriga, Camarines Sur, Philippines. *Primitive Man* 21:65–73.

Macleod, Thomas R. 1972. Verb Stem Classification in Umiray Dumagat. *Philippine Journal of Linguistics* 3(2):43–74.

Masipiqueña, Andres B., Gerard A. Persoon, and Denyse J. Snelder. n.d. [Circa 1999]. The Use of Fire in Northeastern Luzon (Philippines): Conflicting Views of Local People, Scientists, and Government Officials. *Avenir des Peuples des Forets Tropicales.* http://lucy.ukc.ac.uk/Rainforest/ Workingpaperspublic/Fire/fire_TOC.html (June 20, 2002) [16 pages].

Mayfield, Roy. 1972. Agta Sentence Structure [Central Cagayan]. *Linguistics: An International Review* 85:21–66.

Mayfield, Roy. 1983. Some Features of Hortatory Discourse in Central Cagayan Agta. *Studies in Philippines Linguistics* 4(2):88–124. (Linguistic Society of the Philippines and the Summer Institute of Linguistics.)

Mayfield, Roy. 1987. *Central Cagayan Agta Texts.* Studies in Philippine Linguistics (Supplementary Series: Philippine Texts No. 2). Manila: Linguistic Society of the Philippines and Summer Institute of Linguistics.

Mudar, Karen. 1985. Bearded Pigs and Beardless Men: Predator-Prey Relations between Pigs and Agta in Northeastern Luzon, Philippines. In P. Bion Griffin and Agnes A. Estioko-Griffin (eds.), *The Agta of Northeastern Luzon: Recent Studies,* 69–84. Cebu City, Philippines: University of San Carlos Publications.

Nickell, Thomas L. 1985. A Partial Stratification Analysis of Eastern Cagayan Agta Language. In P. Bion Griffin and Agnes A. Estioko-Griffin (eds.), *The Agta of Northeastern Luzon: Recent Studies,* 119–146. Cebu City, Philippines: University of San Carlos Publications.

Nicolaisen, Johannes. 1974–1975. The Negritos of Casiguran Bay: Problems of Affluency, Territoriality and Human Aggressiveness in Hunting Societies of Southeast Asia. *Folk: Dansk Ethnografisk Tidsskrift* 16–17:401–434.

Noval-Morales, Daisy, and James Monan. 1979. *A Primer on the Negritos of the Philippines.* Manila: Philippine Business for Social Progress.

Ogawa, Hidefumi. 1985. Piniobranca Negrito [Penablanca Negrito]. *Ethnos* 27:13–20, 55–73. [Published in Shimonosekishi City, Japan; written in Japanese.]

Perez, Lorenzo. 1928. Los Aetas e Ilongotes de Filipinas: Apendices. *Archivo Ibero-Americano* 15:71–106.

Peterson, Jean. 1976. Folk Traditions and Interethnic Relations in Northeastern Luzon, Philippines. In A. L. Kaeppler and H. A. Nimmo (eds.), *Directions in Pacific Traditional Literature,* 319–330. Honolulu: Bishop Museum Press.

Peterson, Jean. 1977. Ecotones and Exchange in Northern Luzon. In Karl L. Hutterer (ed.), *Economic Exchange and Social Interaction in Southeast Asia,* 55–71. [Ann Arbor], Michigan: Center for South and Southeast Asia Studies.

Peterson, Jean. 1977. The Merits of Margins. In W. Wood (ed.), *Cultural-Ecological Perspectives on Southeast Asia,* 63–73. Athens: Ohio University Center for International Studies.

Peterson, Jean. 1978. Hunter-Gatherer/Farmer Exchange. *American Anthropologist* 80:335–381.

Peterson, Jean. 1978. *The Ecology of Social Boundaries: Agta Foragers of the Philippines.* Urbana: University of Illinois Press.

Peterson, Jean. 1981. Game, Farming, and Interethnic Relations in Northeastern Luzon, Philippines. *Human Ecology* 9(1):1–22.

Peterson, Jean. 1982. The Effect of Farming Expansion on Hunting. *Philippine Sociological Review* 30:33–50.

Peterson, Jean T. 1984. Cash, Consumerism, and Savings: Economic Change among the Agta Foragers of Luzon, Philippines. In Barry L. Isaac (ed.), *Research in Economic Anthropology,* Vol. 6, 53–73. Greenwich: JAI Press.

Peterson, Jean T. 1985. Hunter Mobility, Family Organization and Change. In R. Munsell Prothero and Murray Chapman (eds.), *Circulation in Third World Countries,* 124–144. London: Routledge Kegan Paul.

Peterson, Jean T., and Warren Peterson. 1977. Implication of Contemporary and Prehistoric Exchange Systems. In J. Allen, J. Golson, and R. Jones (eds.), *Sunda and Sahul: Prehistoric Studies in Southeast Asia, Melanesia and Australia,* 533–564, London: Academic Press.

Peterson, Warren. 1974. Summary Report of Two Archaeological Sites from Northeastern Luzon. *Archaeology and Physical Anthropology in Oceania* 9(1):26–35.

Peterson, Warren. 1981. Recent Adaptive Shifts among Palanan Hunters of the Philippines. *Man* 16:4–61.

Philippine Commission. 1908. *Eighth Annual Report of the Philippine Commission, 1907.* Washington, D.C.: Government Printing Office.

Pili, Miguel V. 1979. The Agta of Mount Asog, City of Iriga. Ph.D. dissertation in Education, University of Saint Anthony, City of Iriga, Camarines Sur.

Rahmann, Rudolf. 1984. The Nocturnal Prayer Ceremonies of the Negritos of the Philippines. In M. Bhuriya and S. M. Michael (eds.), *Anthropology as a Historical Science: Essays in Honour of Stephen Fuchs,* 223–240. Indore: Sat Prachar Press.

Rai, Navin K. 1981. Under the Shadow of Soft Gold: The Impact of the Logging Industry on a Hunter-Gatherer Society. *Impulse* 8(1):48–50.

Rai, Navin K. 1982. From Forest to Field: A Study of Philippine Negrito Foragers in Transition. Ph.D. dissertation, Department of Anthropology, University of Hawai'i, Honolulu. Ann Arbor, Mich.: University Microfilms International.

Rai, Navin K. 1985. Ecology in Ideology: An Example from the Agta Foragers of the Philippines. In P. Bion Griffin and Agnes Estioko-Griffin (eds.), *The Agta of Northeastern Luzon: Recent Studies,* 33–44. Cebu City, Philippines: University of San Carlos Publications.

Rai, Navin K. 1990. *Living in a Lean-to: Philippine Negrito Foragers in Transition.* Ann Arbor: Museum of Anthropology, University of Michigan.

Reid, Lawrence A. 1987. The Early Switch Hypothesis: Linguistic Evidence for Contact Between Negritos and Austronesians. *Man and Culture in Oceania* 3 (Special Issue):41–59.

Reid, Lawrence A. 1989. Arta, Another Philippine Negrito Language. *Oceanic Linguistics* 28(1):47–74.

Reid, Lawrence A. 1992. Southeast Asian Linguistic Traditions in the Philippines. Paper presented to the Biennial Conference of the Japan Society of Southeast Asian Historians, Tokyo University, June 13 [14 pages].

Reid, Lawrence A. 1994. Possible Non-Austronesian Lexical Elements in Philippine Negrito Languages. *Oceanic Linguistics* 33:37–72. [The first researcher to find evidence for a non-Austronesian substratum in the languages spoken by Philippine Negritos; hypothesizes that the Negritos developed an early pidgin or trade language, subsequently creolized, that they used to facilitate communication with in-migrating Austronesians.]

Reid, Lawrence A. 1994. Unraveling the Linguistic Histories of Philippine Negritos. In Thomas Dutton and Darrell Tryon (eds.), *Language Contact and Change in the Austronesian World,* 443–475. Berlin: Mouton de Gruyter.

Rosaldo, Renato. 1983. Utter Savages of Scientific Value. In Eleanor Leacock and Richard B. Lee (eds.), *Politics and History in Band Societies,* 309–326. Cambridge: Cambridge University Press.

Schaefer, Judith. 1999. Zur Symbiose von Jaegern und Sammlern mit ihren Nachbarn im tropischen Regenwald. Am Beispiel der Agta. M.A. thesis. Department of Cultural Anthropology, University of Munich, Germany. [Written in German, 150 pp., archived at the U of Munich.]

Schebesta, Paul. 1952. *Die Negrito Asiens,* Vol. I. Wien: Modling.

Schebesta, Paul. 1954. *Die Negrito Asiens,* Vol. II. Wien: Modling.

Schebesta, Paul. 1957. *Die Negrito Asiens,* Vol. II, 2. Wien: Modling.

Scherer, Otto. 1909. Linguistic Traveling Notes from Cagayan (Luzon). *Anthropos* 4:801–804. [Last name of author is spelled elsewhere as Scheerer.]

Semper, Carl. 1861. Reise durch die Nordostlichen Provinzen der Insel Luzon. *Zeitschrift fur Allgemeine Erdkunde,* Vol. 10, 249–266. Berlin: [D. Reimer]. [For partial commentary, see William H. Scott, Semper's 'Kalingas' 120 Years Later. *Philippine Sociological Review* 27(1979):93–101.]

Simangan, Melchor. 1956. The Negritos of Palanan, Isabela: Their Life and Culture. M.A. thesis in Education. National University, Manila.

Simon, S. 1975. The Socioeconomic Status of the Dumagats of Palanan, Isabela:
    Its Implications to Education. M.A. thesis in Education. Northeastern
    College, Santiago.
Simon, S. 1982. The Community Life of the Dumagats of Palanan, Isabela: Its
    Implications to Development, Ph.D. dissertation in Education. St. Paul
    University, Tuguegarao, Cagayan.
Simon, Samuel E. 1988–1989. The Community Life of the Dumagats of
    Palanan, Isabela. *Journal of Northern Luzon* 19(1–2):1–57.
Tamaki, Yasuaki. 1989. Luson-tou hokutoubu no Dumagatto-zoku: Filipin-
    Neguriito Kenkyuu eno ichizuke [Dumagat of Northeastern Luzon, Philip-
    pines: Placing Them in the Research of Philippine Negritos.] [English
    translation of Japanese title.] Minzokugaku Kenkyu *[The Japanese Journal
    of Ethnology]* 53/54(3):399–409. [Written in Japanese.]
Tamaki, Yasuaki. 1999. Interethnic Relations and Identity Politics among the
    [Umiray] Dumagat of Northeastern Luzon: In Terms of the Relation with
    Tagalog and Tingguian. In Toh Goda, ed., *Political Culture and Ethnicity:
    An Anthropological Study in Southeast Asia,* 121–139. Quezon City, Philip-
    pines: New Day.
Turnbull, Wilfred. 1929. The 'Dumagats' of North-East Luzon. *Philippine
    Magazine* 26(3):131–133, 175–178; 26(4):208–209, 237–240.
Turnbull, Wilfred. 1930. Bringing a Wild Tribe under Government Control.
    Philippine Magazine 26(12):782–798; 27(1):31–120; 27(2):90–120.
Vanoverbergh, Morice. 1937. *Some Undescribed Languages of Luzon.*
    Nijmegen: Dekker S. Van de Vegt N.V. Publications de la Commission
    d'Enquete Linguistique, III.
Vanoverbergh, Morice. 1937–1938. Negritos of Eastern Luzon. *Anthropos*
    32:905–928; 33:119–164.
Wastl, J. 1957. Beitrag zur Anthropologie der Negrito von Ost-Luzon. *Anthro-
    pos* 52:769–812.
Worcester, Dean. 1912. Headhunters of Northern Luzon. *National Geographic
    Magazine* 23:833–930.
Worcester, Dean. 1955. *Domestic Economy of the Dumagats.* Pontificia Acca-
    demia delle Scienze (Rome) Acta, Vol. 18.
Zipagang, A. 1970. A Survey of Dumagat Culture in Palanan, Isabela. M.A.
    thesis. University of Santo Tomas, Manila.

Addendum 1: Archival Sources of Agta Music

In the 1960s Thomas Headland and Jose Maceda recorded several pieces of traditional Casiguran Agta music (both songs and instrumental) as well as Palanan Agta music by an anonymous collector. Dr. Maceda was at the time a professor of ethnomusicology at the University of the Philippines. These recordings are deposited in the following three places:

1. The Department of Asian Music, University of the Philippines. For the list, see the Maceda (1975) reference below. Refer to "Agta" on p. 498 and "Dumagat" on p. 509.

2. Peoples of the Pacific Hall, The American Museum of Natural History, New York City.

3. Cantometrics, Apartment 12E, 215 West 98th Street, New York, NY. See Lomax (1971) below.

Lomax, Alan. 1971. A Computerized Output of Casiguran Dumagat [Agta] Song Style, An Evaluation. Unpublished computer output, Cantometrics, Apt. 12E, 215 West 98th Street, New York, NY. Copy in the files of the Philippine Branch of the Summer Institute of Linguistics, Manila.

Maceda, Jose. 1975. A Preliminary List of Vocal Music in the Philippines as Recorded in a Collection of Tapes at the Department of Asian Music, University of the Philippines. In Francisco R. Demetrio (ed.), *Dialogue For Development: Papers from the First National Congress of Philippine Folklore,* Xavier University, Cagayan de Oro, December 1972, 497–548. Cagayan de Oro, Philippines: Xavier University.

Addendum 2: A List of Important Bibliographies on Philippine Negritos

Garvan, John M. 1964. The Negritos of the Philippines (ed. by Hermann Hochegger). Vienna: Verlag Ferdinand Berger Horn (pp. 272–274).

Genet, Varcin, E. 1951. *Les Negritos de L'ile de Lucon, Philippines.* Paris: Societe d'Anthropologie. (See the Bibliographie, pp. 247–256.)

Lebar, Frank, ed. 1975. *Negritos. Ethnic Groups of Insular Southeast Asia: Philippines and Formosa,* Vol. 2, 24–31. New Haven: Human Relations Area Files Press. (References in the bibliography on Negritos are cited in the text.)

Maceda, Marcelino N. 1975. *The Culture of the Mamanua (Northeast Mindanao) as Compared with that of the Other Negritos of Southeast Asia.* 2nd edition. 126–148. Cebu City: University of San Carlos.

Noval-Morales, Daisy Y., and James Moran. 1979. *A Primer on the Negritos of the Philippines,* 180–200. Manila: Philippine Business for Social Progress.

Rahmann, Rudolf. 1975. The Philippine Negritos in the Context of Research on Food-Gatherers during this Century. *Philippine Quarterly of Culture and Society* 3:204–236, (231–234).

Saito, Shiro. 1972. *Philippine Ethnography: A Critically Annotated and Selected Bibliography.* Honolulu: The University Press of Hawai'i. [References to Negritos are scattered throughout the book. Look in Index under "Negrito," "Dumagat," "Batak," etc.]

Warren, Charles P. 1959. Negrito Groups in the Philippines: Preliminary Bibliography. Unpublished typescript. University of Chicago, Philippine Studies Program. (16 pages, contains 258 bibliographic entries. Copy also in the library of the University of the Philippines, Diliman.)

Reviews

A Small Exhibit on the Agta and Their Future
Originally published as a Museum Anthropology review in
American Anthropologist 103(2):515–521 (June 2001)

P. Bion Griffin

The Philippine Agta: Their Rain Forest Is Gone: What Now? International Museum of Cultures, Dallas, TX. March 18, 2000–January 18, 2001.

The Agta exhibit was small, was in a small museum, and was seen by a small number of people, when compared with the large exhibits and museums often reviewed in the *American Anthropologist.* The exhibit, however, carried a large message and was, I believe, important both in its own right and in its exemplification of specialized museums around the world. A few devotees, who reached out in an effective way, telling us of a situation worthy of attention, presented an ethnic group and some of their problems. Professionalism and passion were both present and audiences educated. The exhibit was accompanied by a successful lecture series and a symposium that repeated at the Museum and at Southern Methodist University. The lectures and symposium will be published in *Notes in Anthropology,* an in-house publication of the museum.*

The Agta, their lost forest, and their uncertain future were the exhibit's foci. The Agta are members of a minority group widely scattered through the mountains of eastern Luzon, the northernmost of the major Philippine islands. Through much of the twentieth century Agta were foragers with an emphasis on hunting, fishing, very small-scale swiddening, and trading with neighboring farmers. Phenotypically distinct from most Filipinos, Agta are likely remnants of older populations that entered the Philippine archipelago in the late Pleistocene. Since the end of World War II, the Philippine population has grown on both sides of the mountains, and logging has reached into the furthest tree stands. The basis of Agta economy has deteriorated and changed to a point were one may correctly say, "Their forest is gone: now what?" One of the principal scholars of the Agta, Thomas N. Headland, anthropology consultant with the Summer Institute of Linguistics (SIL), asked that question, being the creative force behind the exhibit at the International Museum of Cultures in Dallas, Texas (http://www.sil.org/imc/exhibits.htm).

---

* Editors' note: After this review was written, the decision was made to publish this book in Publications in Ethnography rather than in *NOA.*

Below I describe and analyze the exhibit, reflecting on the nature and accomplishments of such small and short-lived presentations. First, however, I should place myself within the Agta and the exhibit, allowing the reader to better assess my judgment. My wife, Agnes Estioko-Griffin, and son, Marcus Griffin, and I have lived off and on since 1972 among the Agta, working north of the groups among whom Thomas and Janet Headland and their children resided. Dr. Headland and I have together considered the Agta for decades. In addition, I have worked closely with SIL missionaries since the 1970s. I approached the exhibit with a friendly yet critical eye.

The exhibit begins with a large photographic montage seemingly depicting an Agta man squatting on the edge of a high-rise building. He gazes off over the Makati Commercial Center, Manila's opulent shopping mall. Moving past this image, one is immediately confronted by a massive and striking photo montage which centers the main theme of the exhibit and backs the diorama of an Agta campsite and a single life-size manikin representing a man hard at work starting a fire by the traditional friction method. He stands beside a stream, his back to his "lean-to" shelter, with vegetation edging the rear of the structure. Wild pig jaw trophies hang from an upright pole, and betel nut paraphernalia lie nearby, as does an aluminum cooking pot and baskets. The curved photo montage rises from waist height to the ceiling, drawing the eye away from the manikin and artifacts and to the dramatic change from tropical forest to log pond (a place where unsawed timber is stored before processing or shipment). This montage blends scenes edited from several photographs, fabricating a continuous progression that strikingly highlights the destruction of eastern Luzon's forests and, by extension, the Agta homeland. Larger photographs are placed strategically in each end for the montage. Hunting activities highlight the "forest" end; Agta associated with a logging truck and logger's camp emphasize the "log pond" end. Two horizontal artifact cases and photographic wall displays of Agta compliment the main presentation. The artifact cases are nicely assisted by photographs of, for example, the wearing of the beautiful examples of Agta beadwork. The other photographs present Agta from various Agta dialect groups in eastern Luzon, largely engaged in subsistence activities and around dwellings. Butchering scenes are certainly colorful and titillating for younger audiences.

The professional skill of the museum's Curator of Collections, Gary Eastty, is evident in the design and construction of the material of the exhibit. Working closely with Headland and coping with limited space and resources, Eastty built a very lifelike setting. The Agta man is sculpted with a good eye to proportions. The artifacts and materials used for the dwelling are genuine; the poles and palm fronds used were shipped from the Philippines. Stephen Headland, who learned the craft as a child among the Agta, accurately assembled the lean-to.

Faults can be found, if one is unwilling to attend to the limitations inherent in small spaces and small budgets, and one can reflect on the effectiveness of the desired message's delivery. A single man building a fire with other than matches or a borrowed live ember is a curiosity. A lean-to with but one man and no wife, children, dogs, and bits of rubbish would, I think, amuse any Agta. Everything is so clean! The man's loincloth, his betel pouch, and the baskets are amazingly new, yet the aluminum cooking pot is covered with soot! Truly, the wife is far away, since she would have used the sand lying between the lean-to and the stream for an abrasive as she scoured the pot clean and bright—at least if she knew visitors would be observing her home! The man is clearly a fine hunter, reflecting his pre-log pond life, since a cluster of "trophy" large wild pig jaws hang from the lean-to's upright poles. The diminished forest of today does not house such catches. We have here a simple and straightforward, if a touch idealized or sanitized, presentation of Agta traditional life. I feel certain that Eastty and Headland would share my desire to have an example of an early twenty-first-century Agta woman and her house. This would demonstrate the huge impact of the global economy on Agta culture and material consumption. The lean-to might be missing, replaced by a shabby imitation of a farmer's house. Bows and arrows could be lacking, replaced by a gun or, in an extreme, a chainsaw. Pigs and chickens would be more in evidence than hunting dogs, and the beadwork and loincloth now replaced with secondhand shirts and shorts or trousers. Space limitations precluded a more complex display.

The coupling of the main diorama and the dominant montage, assisted by the photographs, give the viewer a good idea of Agta life before, during, and after forest loss. The view into the future is less effective. The impact of deforestation remains conjectural. The exhibit asks, "What now?" but we, the viewers, can only lament what appears to be a happy people busily engaged in a satisfying way of life. We cannot really assess the impact of changes, even through photographs of Agta working with loggers. Sophisticated viewers do necessarily engage the issue, likely raising their own scenarios as possibilities. Younger audiences, I suspect, leave with one of several impressions—"Wow, interesting, I'd like to visit them," or "How disgusting! How can they live without enough clothes and in such awful houses. Yuck!" Or, most likely, "Where do they go to the bathroom?" At least the photographs of children convey a sense of satisfaction—no wretched, emaciated children stare out at nervous viewers. Few such children can be found among today's Agta. The possible exoticizing of "the other" seems inescapable in the exhibit, and in all the museum's exhibits. Foregrounding the Agta without the presence of anthropologists, missionaries, tourists, government officials, and recent migrants into their lands does leave a gap in understanding and in seeing the complexity of their futures.

The beginnings of answers to "What now?" came to the audiences who attended the lecture series and the symposium attached to the exhibit. The International Museum of Cultures Lecture Series "Cultural Extinction of Indigenous Peoples" ran from May 2 through October 24, 2000. The series permitted in-depth exploration of precisely the "What Now?" question as well as bringing a broad comparative focus to forager futures. The exhibit was kicked off with a lecture at the museum by Dr. Headland. Drawing on his 38 years' association with Agta, he introduced them as "The Philippine Agta: Rainforest People." Headland also closed the exhibit, in association with the Filipino Festival Day at the museum with his address "Indigenous Peoples and Philippine Culture." The museum, through Headland, gave the whole effort distinction by bringing a panel of scholars to Dallas for two days of lectures. The final frosting on the cake is the now in-press renditions of the lectures.

"What place for hunter-gatherers in Millennium Three?" oriented the theme of the panel guest speakers (http://www.sil.org/imc/agta092500.htm). Two performances were held, first at the SIL international headquarters adjacent to the museum and the second, co-sponsored by the SMU Department of Anthropology on September 25, at Southern Methodist University, where a much larger and more diverse audience was reached. The panelists were charged with addressing issues of the disappearance of hunter-gatherer societies, deforestation, and social and economic causes, as well as human rights issues. Headland introduced the topic and the speakers. Dr. Ben Wallace of Southern Methodist University discussed deforestation, reforestation, and related social change. Dr. Sy Sohmer, Director of the Botanical Research Institute of Texas and a specialist on Philippine forests, painted a grim picture of the extent of forest loss. Dr. Robert Bailey of the University of Illinois, Chicago, brought his knowledge of Ituri forest peoples, the Efe and Lese, to bear on the problem, and Dr. Robert Hitchcock of the University of Nebraska contributed insights from his human rights and development work among Kalahari foragers. Dr. Navin Rai of the World Bank discussed his extensive experience in gaining land rights for the Agta, and I reviewed aspects of ongoing Agta adaptation to their changing social and natural environments.

This assembly of experts added depth, breadth, and legitimacy to the museum's efforts, both within and outside of SIL. In addition, the energy created among the panelists brought some measure of renewed commitment to advocacy for the benefit of their host communities. I suspect that the respect tendered between the panelists and the International Museum of Cultures' hosts also went far to increase a sense of positive relations in the larger anthropological and missionary communities. The years of work by SIL anthropologists were, I suspect, further validated by the enthusiasm of the outside scholars.

The International Museum of Cultures is the context in which the Agta exhibit was, albeit briefly, sited, and in which its larger associations must be understood. The museum is entirely an ethnographic museum, designed by and for SIL members who are missionaries, linguists, and anthropologists. These people usually have had very extensive experience among indigenous communities, far more than most academic anthropologists. Their museum's mission statement reads: "To be a window on indigenous people of the world and to create greater appreciation of ethnic and cultural diversity, thereby furthering mutual respect and peace between peoples." Christian proselytizing is not found herein; I saw no copies of the New Testament, translated into Casiguran Agta by the Headlands, in the exhibit. Instead the several ethnographic monographs published on the Agta were on display and sale in the museum shop.

I cannot closely discuss the permanent exhibits in this review, except to comment that they are generally well done, but, as with the Agta exhibit, they minimize or exclude the presence of the observers who eventually produced the final product. Since SIL members are often involved with literacy training, one major exhibit featured the life of a Shipibo boy who gained literacy and became a teacher. His "exhibit" development involved consultation with Shipibo and a visitation from Peru. Children marvel at his life, know he is still alive, and reflect on the changes and struggles he endured. Overall exhibits provide responsible views of several interesting cultures and give Dallas-area guests a comfortable visit. Of course, the museum and the exhibits should be considered as designed by and for the community that produced it. SIL is a large and congenial Christian group with a variety of opinions and agendas, as with any large enduring organization. SIL has long fostered anthropology among its own. Tom Headland is a Senior Anthropological Consultant holding a Ph.D. in anthropology and having major publications to his credit. His special mission drives the message of the exhibit and his commitment to the enhancement of anthropological sensitivity, the collection of anthropological data, and the improvement of the quality of life of the Agta.

The goals and deliveries of small, specialized museums should be of special interest to anthropologists, especially ethnographic efforts by special interest groups that are at times considered outside the boundaries of traditional academic anthropology. And, as diverse organizations around the world adopt the notion that "a museum" is of value, how these are conceived and realized in small places and with small budgets is of more than academic interest. The Agta exhibit at the International Museum of Cultures, independent from yet associated with the Summer Institute of Linguistics, provides one example of the trend. Not without flaws from some points of view, but fitting in with late-twentieth-century attempts to depict positively what to most residents of Dallas are indeed different people, the exhibit raises questions that can be conceptualized by most viewers as relevant to their own lives and futures.

Area Filipinos Help Tell Story of Aborigines

By Katie Menzer Staff Writer of *The Dallas Morning News*[1]

Susie Domagas was a college student in the Philippines 30 years ago when she visited an aboriginal community in the mountains of Luzon. The memories, she says, are still vivid.

"You should have seen where they lived. They had everything they needed in just one room," said Ms. Domagas, president of the Filipino-American Association of Fort Worth. "Their lives are so different from people living in the city. My parents' house has six bedrooms."

Those memories came flooding back recently when Ms. Domagas visited an exhibit at the International Museum of Cultures in Dallas that documents the disappearing aborigine people of the Philippines.

The exhibit, "The Philippine Agta: Their Rainforest is Gone, What Now?" features pictures and artifacts of the Agta Negrito, a nomadic culture of hunters and gatherers living in the rain forest of eastern Luzon's Sierra Madre mountains. Because of deforestation and the Filipino population explosion of the past three decades, anthropologists say, the Agta culture is facing extinction.

The museum's display is part of a continuing series of exhibits on cultures from around the world. Museum officials hope it will draw interest from Filipinos living in the Dallas area.

The exhibit's organizers consulted with some of the area's Filipino residents, and with Dallas anthropologist Dr. Thomas Headland, to create the exhibit.

Emelita de la Rosa, 56, the president of the Philippine Community Center in Carrollton, was one of the community advisers. She said that her work with the exhibit was an eye-opening experience.

"When they said there were Agta people still existed, I myself was surprised," said Ms. de la Rosa, an accountant. "Unless you really live with them, you don't see them."

Dr. Headland, who lived with the Agta people for 24 years, said that most Filipino people know little about the 10,000 Agta Negritos living in the Philippines today.

"It's like the American Indian community here," said Dr. Headland, 64. "How many Americans have been to a reservation to see the miserable conditions in which they live? People just don't know."

Ms. de la Rosa, who emigrated from the Philippines in 1970, estimates about 25,000 Filipinos are scattered throughout the Dallas area. She said many learn English in school in the Philippines and have less trouble assimilating into American culture than other immigrants. Displays like the Agta exhibit are important to her community to help them keep their culture alive, she said.

---

[1] Published May 7, 2000 and reprinted with permission of *The Dallas Morning News*

The exhibit details the Agta's history and the reasons for their decline. Its culture has undergone an abrupt and massive transformation in the past 30 years. Because of logging and mining, only 3 percent of the hardwood rain forest that supported the Agta exists today, Dr. Headland said. And an urban population explosion has forced Filipinos to clear land for farms and other developments.

Dr. Headland and his wife, Janet, joined the Casiguran Agta, a small group of Agta people living along rivers in the mountains of the northeastern Luzon coast, in 1962. They raised their three children amid the Agta society, watching it change from a culture of hunter-gatherers to one of peasant workers laboring on nearby farms.

Dr. Headland said that a growing percentage of the Agta women are marrying outside the society, moving out of the rain forest to live on their husband's farms. He believes the Agta culture will soon vanish from the Philippines.

"As an anthropologist, I can't help but be saddened to see the demise of a way of life that was adaptive for thousands of years just disappear in 50 years," Dr. Headland said.

Ms. de la Rosa said she is also saddened but is grateful that the exhibit exists to educate both Filipinos and non-Filipinos about the unfamiliar Agta culture.

"These people don't have homes and our children here do have homes," Ms. de la Rosa said. "It makes us appreciate what we have."

The International Museum of Cultures is a small, independent museum on the campus of SIL International, an organization whose members work worldwide with indigenous groups on linguistic analysis and Bible translation.

The museum is at 7500 W. Camp Wisdom Road. For more information, call the museum at 972-708-7406.

Index

SIL International
The International Museum of Cultures
Publications in Ethnography

Recent Publications

For further information or a full listing of SIL publications contact:

International Academic Bookstore
SIL International
7500 W. Camp Wisdom Road
Dallas TX 75236-5699

Voice: 972-708-7404
Fax: 972-708-7363
Email: academic_books@sil.org
Internet: http://www.ethnologue.com